108

Reading "KIM" Right

Reading "KIM" Right

Frank Davey

Vancouver • Talonbooks • 1993

Published with the assistance of the Canada Council

Talonbooks
201 / 1019 East Cordova Street
Vancouver, British Columbia V6A 1M8
Canada

This book was typeset in Palatino by Pièce de Résistance Ltée., and printed and bound in Canada by Hignell Printing Ltd.

First printing: June 1993

Canadian Cataloguing in Publication Data

Davey, Frank, 1940-
Reading "Kim" right

Includes bibliographical references.
ISBN 0-88922-342-4

1. Campbell, Kim, 1947- 2. Cabinet ministers—Canada—Biography. 3. Politicians—Canada—Biography. 4. Press and politics—Canada. I. Title.
FC631.C34D39 1993 971.064'7'092
F1034.3.C34D39 1993 C93-091582-8

Contents

CHAPTER I

Who is "Kim Campbell"

"Who is 'Kim Campbell'?" The question appeared in the Canadian newspapers in late March 1993, as Avril Phaedra "Kim" Campbell began her campaign to succeed Brian Mulroney as leader of the Progressive Conservative party and Prime Minister of Canada. The question did not imply a mysterious identity. Nor did it quite mean that Campbell might be a "Joe Who," a nonentity who might not deserve the Tory leadership. The media were well-acquainted with the small blonde woman who had been elected Member of Parliament for Vancouver Centre in 1988, named Minister of Justice in 1990, and Minister of Defence in January 1993. In fact, many in the media had gazed perhaps more intently than they should have at this woman, whose ostensibly 'nude' image, bare-shouldered behind legal robes, they had published repeatedly in late 1992 and early 1993, and whose controversial, subliminally 'sexy' legislative forays as Minister of Justice — an abortion bill, a "rape-shield" law, gun control regulations, a bill to protect homosexual rights — they had featured in numerous front-page stories. Rather, the question was about policy, a coy question that asked that "Kim Campbell" be the code word for some dramatic new politics — a new Canada, perhaps, in which Canadians smiled and prospered, or a new economics in which Canadians miraculously enjoyed low taxes and generous social programmes. It was, at the very least, a request that "Kim Campbell" mean something much different from "Brian Mulroney" and the recession-plagued Canada he appeared to have created.

"Who is 'Kim Campbell'?" Campbell repeated this question back to her audiences in the opening week — March 26-April 2 — of her leadership campaign, insisting that she was indeed as politically different as she was, in her emphatic blondness and femaleness, visually different. She was already, she insisted, 'known' — both through the legislation with which she had been associated and through the manner in which she had steered it through Parliament and its committees. She would propose specific policies in good time. She would, moreover, "rethink government." She would "change the way we do politics." She would employ an "open and representative" approach to making Senate appointments. Despite these declarations, however, questions about the Campbell identity persisted. On April 3, Alberta columnist Kenneth Whyte wrote that Campbell's proposals were mere "sloganeering" and that support for her was an "infatuation" that was "already ... growing thin." On April 8, *The Globe and Mail*'s Ross Howard was suggesting that "[f]or all the talk about her being new and different, Kim Campbell has embarked on a highly traditional campaign." Television and newspaper responses to Campbell's performance in the April-May leadership debates continued this theme. Campbell's responses lacked "substance"; they were "short on specifics"; she offered "generalities" rather than detailed policies; she was nervous about creating controversy.

"What do we know of Kim Campbell?" *The Globe and Mail* asked in a March 26 editorial. The media apparently expected to know not only what the name meant but what the actual small blonde woman might 'do' with Canada once installed as Prime Minister. They wanted explicit declarations, like George Bush's "read my lips — no new taxes," or Mulroney's 1984 "no free trade," by which they could translate a woman's name into predictable policy. The *Globe* could vaguely detect many of the things associated with Campbell that had contributed to her initial popularity. Howard noted that she was "young, female, and a neophyte MP." Its editorial writers noticed a little more, but thought these matters trivial, and went on to hope once more for news on "where she stands."

> She is 46 years old. She's from British Columbia. She has a B.A. in political science. She did not complete a degree at the London School of Economics, taught politics, took law in her thirties, sat on the Vancouver school board, worked for the Social Credit party. She served two years in the B.C. legislature before jumping to federal politics. She is bright and funny, and considers herself an intellectual. She speaks passable French. She changed her name at age 12. She photographs well. That's about it. ("Kim Campbell, for all we know")

Yet in the history of what Canadians have known about their politicians this is not an inconsiderable amount, and in many ways more 'telling' — as the subsequent chapters of this book will explore — than the *Globe* writer seemed to realize. In fact, is it appropriate to expect to know more than this, when politicians themselves don't seem to know much about what policies they may embrace a month, a year, or three years into the future? Do verbal declarations 'say' more about a person than do the kinds of friends they've made or regions they've lived in? Can people remain, as circumstances change, the people they say they are? Did Bush really 'know' he would raise taxes? Did Ontario's NDP Premier Bob Rae anticipate, when he promised voters a government-run automobile insurance company, that he would decide on a contrary policy a few short months after being elected? Did either he or the businessmen who campaigned against him expect him to attempt to roll back the wages of unionized public employees within three years of taking office? Did Alberta Premier Ralph Klein expect to cancel his own legislative pension? Did a libertarian Pierre Trudeau anticipate invoking the War Measures Act? Did Brian Mulroney plan all along to introduce free trade? Can even Kim Campbell, or Avril Phaedra Campbell, or even Defence Minister Campbell, answer the question "Who is Kim Campbell?"

In the academic world, what *Reading "KIM" Right* does would be called "discourse analysis." The book asserts the meaning of a phrase like "Kim Campbell" is social and collective; this meaning is to be found not by looking for "who" the phrase refers to, but by looking in the written history of Canadian culture for the stories and images that have become attached to it. The search for these stories and images will take the book not only into the recent political history of Canada but also into Canada's literature and pop culture. To come to an understanding of "Kim Campbell," we may also have to understand a variety of other popular Canadian stories, from Anne of Green Gables to Margaret Trudeau.

The recurring question of this book, then, is not the journalistic "Who is Kim Campbell," but the more pragmatic "Who is 'Kim Campbell'?" That is, its question is not the imponderable one of who is this flesh-and-blood person and what does she say she will do, but rather what does this currently magical phrase "Kim Campbell" mean, here, in Canada, in the spring and summer of 1993? Voters never vote for flesh-and-blood people, any more than lovers embrace them. It is words and images we vote for and embrace, words and images that move us, because somehow they connect us with what we and our culture have lived with, learned, helped build, come to distrust, believe in, detest, or yearn for. Often the images connect to the persona in ways that outrun and surprise the person they apparently belong to. "It's happening so fast," Campbell observed on the day she declared her candidacy, confessing herself to be "uncomfortable" with her sudden rise to popularity. Perhaps she too was beginning to wonder not only who she was, but also who this stranger was, both beside her and within her, this extraordinary phenomenon — "Kim Campbell."

Photo: Canapress

CHAPTER II

She Named Herself "Kim"

> George Campbell said of his daughter, "I think of Kim as a 12-year old girl with red braids going off to school." ("PC Leadership Notebook," *The London Free Press)*

The most widely cited fact about Kim Campbell's early life is that, at age twelve, she renamed herself "Kim." Why should this fact so interest Campbell commentators? At first glance it seems perhaps no more than an amusing and humanizing juvenile act, an early and endearing act of self-assertion and independence. The renaming, however, enters almost every brief Campbell biography, even the dismissive one in *The Globe and Mail*. Is it the name she chooses that is so engaging, or is it the act of daring itself — of daring to dismiss parentally-given names, of daring to take on the responsibility herself for naming her own identity? Who is "Kim Campbell"? Evidently not a name that even the parents of Avril Phaedra Campbell knew before 1959.

To begin to try to unravel these questions, one should note at the outset that the act of self-naming and self-defining has been loaded with meaning throughout human history. Its overtones of self-caused existence, of being an uncreated "first" — an absolute point on which later people and events base their authenticity — have made this act a part of numerous stories of gods and heroes. The Judaeo-Christian god is described by theologians as always having existed, as an "unmoved mover." Venus is born from the sea, arriving on a Botticelli cockleshell, fully formed. Athena emerges, similarly fully formed, from Zeus' forehead. In Christian tradition, Christ pre-exists his own incarnation, achieving not identity but only bodily form at his birth by way of Mary; the logic of the Trinity, in fact, makes him his own father. "That which exists through itself is what is called meaning," declares the sixth-century Chinese philosopher Lao Tzu. In contemporary India, thousands of Hindu pilgrims trudge a fifty kilometer trail from the Himalayan town of Pahalgam to see and touch a phallus-shaped mound of ice because, like several similar Hindu *lingam*, it appears to be a self-existent object. In the mythology of the United States, early self-defining acts are particularly treasured — Davy Crockett's alleged killing of a bear "when he was only three," or George Washington's refusal to "tell a lie" about the demise of a cherry tree. The "great person" in Western culture is often more believable if he or she has been a child prodigy — revealing his or her worth and special identity at a young age when other less remarkable children show limited understanding and talent. Mozart declares his musicianship when he is six. Alexander Pope writes *Windsor Forest* when he is sixteen. Napoleon is a general of the French army by age twenty-four, and ruler of France by thirty.

■

She danced up to the little looking-glass and peered into it. Her pointed freckled face and solemn gray eyes peered back at her.

"You're only Anne of Green Gables," she said earnestly, "and I see you, just as you are looking now, whenever I try to imagine I'm the Lady Cordelia. But

> it's a million times nicer to be Anne of Green Gables than Anne of nowhere in particular, isn't it?" (Montgomery, *Anne of Green Gables* 65)

In Canadian culture, perhaps to Campbell's good fortune, the self-defining child has most often been female. The most famous of these has been Lucy Maud Montgomery's melodramatic little redhead from Prince Edward Island, the precocious gamin who in making herself "Anne of Green Gables" gave herself not only a name but also, like such ladies of medieval history and legend as Eleanor of Acquitaine and Marie de Champagne, an aristocratic-sounding connection to a place. Here the child is not miraculously born but, like Cinderella, miraculously reborn. She is an orphan, someone who has lost the legitimacy and power of family. But our redhead will eventually succeed in re-establishing her worth and independence not merely to her home community but to millions of weepy-eyed readers, theatre-goers, and TV-viewers. Her elderly adoptive mother Marilla has doubts that she will ever be anything but the misbehaving, rebellious, and clumsy child an orphan is expected to be. But Anne refuses both the orphan stereotype and the model of a pious, unadventurous lady Marilla offers her. She will have her own identity, and will imagine and define her own worthiness in unconventional ways. Her success resonates with the successes of earlier child-heroes who, with their birth-stories hidden, must personally re-create and establish their individual value: young Arthur, pulling the royal sword from the stone, or clumsy Sir Percival, innocently achieving the Holy Grail. Precocious, at least by the standards of rural P.E.I., Anne overwhelms with her wit and charm a succession of stolid, often bitter older women — Marilla, her busybody neighbour Rachel Lynde, the wealthy Josephine Barry — and recalls them to goodness and generosity. Although unschooled until eleven years old, by sixteen she has won a scholarship to college and outshone a professional elocutionist in public recitation. In less than six years she reshapes herself from a pathetic orphan into a self-supporting young woman who can generously repay Marilla for her own impulsive generosity.

The extraordinariness of the orphan — marked by miracles, red-hair, and melodrama — contrasts throughout Montgomery's book with the ordinariness of conventional birth — with the ordinariness of Anne's best friend, Diana Barry, or of her boyfriend-to-be, Gilbert Blythe. In the Conservative leadership campaign, it was the extraordinariness associated with "Kim Campbell" — bright blonde hair, outspokenness, an unconventional childhood, two marriage failures — that rendered emphatically ordinary the much younger Jean Charest. This contrast between the extraordinary and the familiar on June 13 virtually split the delegates and party in two. Although young, Charest appeared next to Campbell to be not a prodigy but merely unusually old. "[A] wholly conventional politician, a kind of francophone Bill Davis," suggested Richard Gwyn in his June 11 column. Far from being self-named, he had not even been named by his parents. André Picard had explained,

> ... the newborn Mr. Charest was supposed to be baptized John James Charest, but the Roman Catholic Québécois priest opted for the more familiar Jean. The decision may have had something to do with his birthday, June 24, Québec's 'national holiday,' St. Jean Baptiste Day.

This naming linked him with institutional continuity, much like his father's background in professional hockey linked him to a more folkloric Quebec sign of continuity. Usually accompanied by his wife (in the *Maclean's* cover photo of June 7 almost enveloped by her) and often surrounded by family members, he presented visually the opposite of orphanhood — family loyalty, the descent of generations, legitimate succession. His surprising success in campaigning against Campbell lay in how easily he wore these familiar signs and fulfilled the traditional leadership images of legitimacy, continuity, maturity and fatherliness — in how comfortable he could appear in a grey suit, a team manager's jacket, and the simplifying rhetoric of a "stump" politician. "A conventional politician; a younger smoother version of the men who have governed this country for the past 126 years," concluded columnist Carol Goar in the *Toronto Star* on June 12.

■

> From a little girl in a broken home to potential prime minister, Kim Campbell's life has the earmarks of political legend. (*The Toronto Star* 1 May, 1993)

What I am suggesting here is not that "Kim Campbell" is another Anne of Green Gables, but rather that aspects of the Anne Shirley story echo both in Canadian memory and in the public perception of "Kim." For this story of the sensitive young woman who doesn't somehow `belong' in the environment into which she has found herself situated, who must somehow refuse to be limited by her birth-identity, who creates for herself a new identity more appropriate to her "finer" qualities, occurs again and again in Canadian writing after *Anne of Green Gables*. Many tellings of this story have become standard material for the Canadian school curriculum. And three of their authors, in particular — Margaret Laurence, Alice Munro, and Margaret Atwood — have themselves become national icons of hard-won selfhood, not unlike the little island redhead. One of the most widely read of Munro's books, *Lives of Girls and Women*, contains the story of Del Jordan, an imaginative and poetic young woman much like Anne, who grows up on a run-down fox farm on the outskirts of a small Ontario town. She is repeatedly embarrassed by both her poverty and by her mother's pretentious eccentricities and, through her sense of personal difference from everyone around her, is able to envision all of them as exotic strangers. Another instance of this story occurs in Atwood's comic novel *Lady Oracle*, which offers an urban version of the same sense of psychological orphanhood in Joan Delacourt, who grows up with a self-absorbed, insecure mother and an aloof and virtually absent father. Joan's attempts to redefine and rename herself are even more extravagant than those of Anne. As a child she eats compulsively to thwart her mother's hopes that she will be a conventionally attractive child. As a young adult she adopts the name of her dead aunt, Louisa K. Delacourt, in order to flee her parents. Later she uses this as both a pen-name under which to secretly write women's novels, and as an identity under which to flee her husband.

Margaret Laurence has given Canadians two powerful, widely-read presentations of a girl embarrassed by her home and family and determined, through intellect and education, to understand her embarrassment and work out her own personal sense of who she is. In *A Bird in the House*, young Vanessa MacLeod finds herself living her childhood and teenage years in her grandparents' houses — brick houses made dark and oppressive by European memories, class pretensions, and by the bitter emotions of her paternal grandmother and maternal grandfather. The inability of her parents to give Vanessa her own home makes her feel, at least spiritually, an orphan from her earliest memories. This feeling is intensified when her father dies when she is twelve years old. Throughout, Laurence depicts Vanessa as feeling both alienated from most other members of her family, and yet uncomfortably similar.

In Laurence's *The Diviners*, Morag Gunn's parents die of fever, much like the birth parents of Montgomery's

Anne. Also like Anne, Morag is too young to remember them. She grows up feeling literally alien to her own family — an orphan, but an orphan who has fallen into circumstances much different from Anne's. Morag has been adopted by the town garbage man and his obese and silent wife. Although neither Vanessa nor Morag renames herself, both aspire to be writers. As children, both use pencils and scribblers to write themselves romantic new identities as an Egyptian princess or a heroic pioneer. Both use their literacy to escape Manawaka for Winnipeg and university study. For both, the perspective of university study helps them to reconcile their childhood inheritances with the new people they have adventured to become. Morag further distances herself from Manawaka by marrying one of her British-born English professors at university, but later divorces him when she realizes that his expectations restrict her search for identity even more than did the poverty of her childhood.

The resemblances between these mythic Canadian stories and the few public facts of the Campbell biography are striking. Like Anne Shirley, who repeatedly laments the ugliness of her red hair, Kim Campbell is born a redhead. Like Vanessa MacLeod, Campbell 'loses' a parent when she is twelve years old. "Her mother ran away from home in 1959, working on yachts in the Mediterranean and the Caribbean for six years before returning to British Columbia, re-married" *Alberta Report* summarizes. This is the year in which Campbell (one year older than Anne Shirley was when she renamed herself) replaces her given names "Avril Phaedra" with "Kim." Like Joan Delacourt she has a father, *Toronto Star* columnist Judy Steed tells us, who is "cold and controlling." Steed's account of the mother's departure emphasises the child's orphan-like desolation: the mother leaves her daughters, not to "see them for almost a decade ... Kim was a vulnerable teenager, estranged from her father who was involved in an affair with a much younger woman named Ginny."

Like the heroines of the stories by Montgomery, Munro, Laurence, and Atwood, Campbell appears, after this crisis, to have a troubled and ambiguous relationship to authority. She and her sister remain, Steed says, "estranged from their father for many years." Campbell declines his financial assistance with her university studies, preferring, according to Michel Vastel of *L'actualité*, "to finance her studies by packing halibut fillets, filling mayonnaise jars, and selling pyjamas and night-gowns." Yet as a sophomore, Steed suggests, she had already "set her cap for Nathan Divinsky ..., a chess master and Gilbert and Sullivan fan who was a math professor at the UBC and 22 years older than she." The orphan rebels against the authorities she encounters in her life, dramatically asserts independence, yet at the same time longs for normality and structure. "It gives me that pleasant ache again just to think of coming really truly home," says Anne Shirley. Anne chafes at arbitrary rules and traditions, yet longs for legitimacy and recognition — to have puffed sleeves like the other girls at the Avonlea Sunday School. Morag resents the rigid class structure of Manawka that views her as wild and uncouth, yet takes special pleasure in being hired as a teenage clerk by a fashionable women's clothing store, and in having "noble" ancestors from the Scottish highlands. Later she will take similar pleasure in being courted by one of her English professors. In the "Campbell" narrative, while a rejection of authority is enacted in her dismissal of her given names, the ambivalent search for it is also enacted when in 1972, like Morag, she marries a professor much older than herself (Divinsky), whom she meets while a student, but later separates from him, again like Morag, as her own professional career develops. This ambivalence is also noticeable in her being reportedly "estranged" from her father, lawyer George Campbell, during her teen years, yet much later enrolling in law school and taking up his profession. Such ambivalence will appear again and again as her career develops.

■

> Marilla was a tall, thin woman, with angles and without curves; her dark hair showed some gray streaks and was always twisted up in a hard little knot behind with two wire hair-pins stuck aggressively through it. She looked like a woman of narrow experience and rigid conscience.... (*Anne of Green Gables* 5)

> That house in Manawaka is the one which, more than any other, I carry with me. Known ... as the Brick House, it was plain as the winter turnips in its root cellar, sparsely windowed as some crusaders' embattled fortress in a heathen wilderness, its rooms in a perpetual gloom except in the brief height of summer. (*A Bird in the House* 3)

The drama that these Canadian books give their young women — depicting them as pulled in one direction by independence, self-assertion, and by a distaste for a past which they view as rigid and imprisoning, and pulled in another by their desire for recognition by authority — is today the drama of Kim Campbell's political life. Self-defined as a rebel of the Canadian right — as the young back-bencher in the B.C. legislature who opposed her Social Credit government's anti-abortion legislation; as the brat who, in running for the Socred leadership, dared to characterize front-runner Bill Vander Zalm as a man whose charisma was "without substance" and therefore "dangerous" — she is also a person who twice has chosen to join political parties already in power. Her twice linking herself with established authority, joining in 1986 a Social

Credit party which had dominated B.C. politics since 1952, and in 1988 a federal party which enjoyed one of the largest parliamentary majorities in Canadian history, in a sense amusingly parallels Morag Gunn's marriage to her English professor and Campbell's own marriages to older men, first to Divinsky and then in 1986 to a lawyer about whose identity the media cannot yet agree. ("Howard Eddy, a laconic, Licolnesque lawyer" writes Judy Steed and most other reporters; "an American-born lawyer, Ronald Whitman" writes Michel Vastel.) Today this drama is repeated in Campbell's billing herself as a bringer of a "new" and "open" way to "do politics" at the same time as she has recruited many of the Conservative party's male authority figures — Marcel Masse, Gilles Loiselle, Lowell Murray, Patrick Kinsella, Jean-Yves Lortie — to advise or direct her campaign.

■

> "I am to pray to Bibi Miriam and I am a Sahib" — he looked at his boots ruefully. "No, I am Kim. This is the great world and I am only Kim. Who is Kim?" He considered his own identity, a thing he had never done before, till his head swam. (Rudyard Kipling, *Kim* 100)

There is no reason to ask or speculate why Campbell should have chosen "Kim" to be the name of her life. In a sense her own motivations here are irrelevant. What influences Canadians today in responding to "Kim Campbell" is not the meaning the name may once have had for her, but the meaning it has for them. For some journalists, the name and the 1959 date of its choosing have evoked Kim Novak, the moderately successful blonde Hollywood actress of the Monroe-Mansfield era. Like the names of many Hollywood actors, the "Kim" of Kim Novak is itself a replacement for a parentally given name, Marilyn. The

"Kim" of Kim Novak is associated with the actress' closely cropped hair, and with the near-masculine overtones in her screen image — an image of understated strength that contrasted strongly with the pliant images of Monroe and Mansfield. At a more general level, "Kim" suggests informality, a nickname rather than a formal name. It operates to deny formality and inheritance, and to suggest accessibility by implying that its bearer is unencumbered by family ties or history.

It is this meaning which the name carries in its most widely known instance (particularly in the ex-British Empire) — as the name of the title character of Rudyard Kipling's 1901 novel. Here "Kim" is again an adopted name, the "street" name of Kimball O'Hara, the orphaned son of a British Army sergeant major, who has been abandoned in India. Kim grows up in the back alleys of Lahore, speaking Urdu and Hindi, and is so browned from the sun that he can pass for a low-caste Hindi boy. In early adolescence he is discovered and given an English education by the British, and recruited for their Secret Service. But although he willingly works for the Crown, he prefers to live barefoot in low-caste Indian dress, with the horse-trader Mahbub Ali, or the itinerant holy man, Teshoo Lama. The ambiguities associated with Kipling's Kim echo and re-echo those that run through the stories of Anne Shirley, Vanessa MacLeod, Morag Gunn, Joan Delacourt, and "Kim Campbell." Like all of them, Kipling's Kim exists in a fierce tension between the white "Sahib" world of his birth, whose restraints and discipline he detests, and the adventurous street life he has made for himself. He has become alien to the authoritative culture of his family. He has symbolically rejected that family both in naming himself Kim and in continually preferring to roam India barefoot with the Lama than to wear boots and attend an English school. Yet like Vanessa MacLeod, who understands she will always carry a part of her grandfather's "Brick House" with her, Kim remains unquestioningly loyal to imperial Britain, eagerly risking his life to act as a spy in her interests.

"Kim" continues today to carry most of the associations it carries in Kipling's *Kim*. It is an androgynous name, a name from boys' adventures, a "tomboy" name both in the earlier male and later female meanings of that word. It is a colloquial name, a street name, which replaces the formality and gender-specificity of the given name — the "Kimball" of Kipling's character, the "Marilyn" of Novak, the "Avril Phaedra" of Campbell. It is a name from the colonies which denies the white European inheritance argued by the names it replaces — in Campbell's case the "avril" of the French calendar, and the tragic Phaedra of Greek myth. It is a name that appears to argue, then, with patriarchy and its authoritative masculine ways of organizing society and enforcing discipline — with the forced wearing of boots by boys and men, and with the obligatory seductiveness of Monroe and Mansfield. It suggests again the openness and newness with which the politician Campbell has been associated. In her case it specifically replaces the Greek Phaedra, mythological daughter of King Minos, who was kidnapped and married by the Greek minotaur-slayer Theseus, and who hanged herself after falling in love with his son Hippolytus. What modern woman, one might ask, wouldn't prefer to name herself "Kim"?

But the question continues to arise: is this "Kim Campbell" really a Kim or does she remain a Phaedra? Is she new, or is she, as Sheila Copps has quipped, "a Mulroney in skirts"? Is she her own self-named woman, or merely a woman all too willing to associate herself with powerful men and conservative masculinist political doctrines? Is she really self-named, a fishpacker and pyjama seller, or is she still, like the mythological Phaedra, the daughter of a man of law, and the dominated wife of a man of authority? "A fresh face?" asks *The Globe and Mail*. "In her corner one finds such haggard devotees to politics-as-usual as Norm Atkins, Larry Grossman, Bill Neville, and Pat Kinsella. Even Dalton Camp shows up, writing fawning newspaper columns in her praise." "Less than meets the eye," suggests *Alberta Report*. The name "Kim Campbell" promised something new, a renaming for a person, a rebirth for a political party, a "new way" of "doing politics" for a country. But the person Kim Campbell had chosen her father's career. Her first political office, in 1980, was the seat on the Vancouver School Board that had just been vacated by her husband. Her first provincial political position was as unelected assistant to B.C. Social Credit Premier Bill Bennett. And in 1993, after she finally declared her candidacy for the Conservative leadership, there were numerous rumours that Brian Mulroney himself had been arranging the stage for her dramatic entry.

Photo: Canapress

CHAPTER III

British Columbia: "Le pays de Kim Campbell"

> Canada's next prime minister will be an admitted marijuana user — a violator of the Narcotic Control Act. (Editorial, *The Toronto Star*, 18 April 1993)

One of the first images of a younger Kim Campbell to be published after she announced her leadership candidacy was a photograph of her playing a guitar in 1970 in Vancouver at age twenty-three. Within a few weeks the photo reappeared in several newpapers in the form of a Jack Lefcourt cartoon entitled "Politicians in their College Years." Here Campbell was depicted with similar guitar and books, but now wearing black tights and holding a smouldering joint of marijuana.

For the cartoonist, the photo had evidently recalled the North American counter-culture of the 1960s and 70s, a period when the flat-topped acoustic guitar was the instrument of both folk music revival and social protest, when coffee-houses such as Vancouver's The Inquisition and The Black Spot were centres for folk music and black-garbed students. Guitar-playing folk artists like Joan Baez, Woody Guthrie, Peter Paul and Mary, and the Kingston Trio were flash-points for youth-led American campaigns against racially segregated schools, the Vietnam War, militarism, and consumerist economics. Along with Toronto and its Yorkville Avenue and Rochdale College, Vancouver was one of the two major Canadian counter-culture centres, a mecca for students across the country who could be seen throughout the springs and summers of the late 60s and early 70s in clusters along the nation's highways, with backpacks, guitars, raised thumbs, and hand-lettered signs reading "Vancouver." Outdoor youth-rallies — the "be-ins" or "love-ins" — in which thousands of young men and women played guitars under the trees, like Campbell in the photograph, listened to music, smoked marijuana, "dropped" LSD and, in their own minds at least, acted out the possibility of a peaceful, loving, communal humanity, were held in Vancouver's Stanley Park. Poet Dan McLeod's *The Georgia Straight* became Canada's most provocative and widely circulated counter-culture newspaper. In editions that often sold more than 30,000 copies, it lobbied for the legalization of marijuana, celebrated "free love," explicitly acknowledged the local homosexual community and its art, and repeatedly accused the Vancouver police of systemic violence against gays and young people. Associated with *The Georgia Straight* was another poet, Stan Persky, who launched a highly public, radical career in student politics at a "tent-in" protest against inadequate student housing, at the University of British Columbia in 1966, and served controversially on the University of British Columbia student council in the late 60s at the same time as Kim Campbell served on that council. Persky went on to found a left-wing counter-culture press, New Star Books, in the early 70s, to edit issues of *The Georgia Straight*'s literary supplement, and to write a number of political books attacking B.C. Social Credit dominance, including a sardonic study of Bill Bennett, *Son of Socred*.

Take away the guitar and the outdoor scene from this

photo, however, and there is no sign left of such an open, adventurous, and radical world. Campbell's hair appears to have been shaped in a middle-class salon. Her skirt is neither a risque mini nor an ankle-length Indian cotton favored by many of the most seriously anticonsumerist young women of the time. Her knees appear to be enclosed in dark-toned nylons. The books in front of her, one of them open as if being read, suggest not someone taking up the guitar as a radical, antiestablishment act, but someone momentarily interrupting dutiful study. Even with the guitar, a close look can lead to doubt about the accuracy of the caption over which *The Globe and Mail* published it, "Kim Campbell plays guitar." Her left hand is forming a C-chord; her right hand appears still; her eyes are focused on the camera lens. If she is playing, she is strumming a standard chord, one apparently taken from the book that is open before her. Moreover, there is no indication of other people in the photo. The guitar of the 1960s was above all a social instrument, played at gatherings where people shared in the singing and in the social messages of the music. The Campbell guitar, in contrast, seems almost asocial. The close focus of the camera insists on her as an individual. It excludes the possibility of other people on that lawn or beside that bush. The young woman herself appears oblivious to the possible presence of anyone except the person holding the camera. She is preoccupied by the fact that she is being photographed, and that the guitar she holds will be part of the image that she and the camera are jointly composing. Twenty years later a *Toronto Star* columnist would report that her declaration that she was running for the Tory leadership was being delayed to allow her to "use the Vancouver Trade Centre with the Coastal Range mountains as a backdrop when she makes her announcement on live television" (Doyle, 22 March 1993).

■

The guitar in the 1970 photograph belongs to the same set of meanings — openness, spontaneity, youthfulness, rebellious concern with social justice — as does an even more widely-circulated image of Kim Campbell, alluded to in the Lefcourt cartoon: the image of her smoking marijuana as a 1965-69 UBC undergraduate. Newspapers across Canada have linked her 1990 admission to the *Cranbrook Daily Townsman*, and a similar admission by fellow Tory leadership candidate Jean Charest, with a generational change in Canadian politics that parallels the change in the United States from the presidency of George Bush to that of Bill Clinton. The two Canadians, it is implied, may be even more radical than Clinton: while he claims to have smoked up only once, and not to have inhaled, the Canadians make no such disclaimer.

The guitar and the marijuana are also tied to general associations in Canadian culture of British Columbia with adventure, iconoclasm, eccentricity, laid-back lifestyles, and bizarre, larger-than-life politicians. Nationally British Columbia is known as Lotus Land, home of nude bathing at Vancouver's Wreck Beach; of Canada's only surfing on Vancouver Island's Long Beach; of megaprojects like the Crowsnest coal fields and Kitimat's Alcan smelters. It is the "Super Natural" land of government travel commercials: rivers silver and red with salmon; mountains covered in powder snow for helicopter skiing; killer whales leaping to entertain cruise ship passengers. It is the home province of Maggie Sinclair-Trudeau, another political daughter known to have smoked marijuana, whose semi-nude exploits were rumoured to have taken her at least as far as the back seat of a limo rented by the 1960s' ultimate rock band, The Rolling Stones. B.C. is the other California, the gold rush province, the last frontier, gateway to the Orient, the fastest-growing province, the

Canadian last place of opportunity, the chosen destination for most of Canada's internal migration.

Politically, as the Margaret Trudeau images insist, British Columbia resonates in Canada as the province of excess. Here William A. Smith, who anticipated and outdid the twelve-year-old Avril Phaedra Campbell by grandiloquently renaming himself, at age twenty-nine, "Amor de Cosmos" (by an act, no less, of the California senate), became the province's second premier in 1872. The premier from 1900 to 1902, coal magnate James Dunsmuir, expended much of his fortune to build a stone castle more extravagant than the Victorian folly, also in stone, built by his father. Earlier, in partnership with his father in 1889, Dunsmuir had persuaded the province to pay the family $750,000 plus one-quarter of Vancouver Island to build a railroad which would connect the Dunsmuir's Nanaimo collieries to the harbour and British naval base at Esquimalt. The B.C. Premier from 1952 to 1972 was W.A.C. "Wacky" Bennett, an audacious politician who, after resigning from a coalition Liberal-Conservative caucus in 1951, simultaneously joined and founded a "Social Credit" party and led it to victory a year later. Bennett's two decades of power were marked by dramatic multi-million dollar decisions: the nationalization of the province's ferry system in 1958, and of its hydro-electric power system in 1961, the extension of the PGE Railway and the hydro-electric development of the Peace and Columbia rivers in the later 1960s. His successors included his son Bill Bennett, charged with insider-trading shortly after resigning in 1986, and Bill Vander Zalm, who left office under a cloud after appearing to use his influence as premier to sell his Biblical theme park to an Asian investor.

■

> "When you come right down to it, he's a bigot." (Campbell, speaking of Bill Vander Zalm's proposals to de-fund abortions in 1988)

While British Columbia carries, nationally, a strong image of extravagance — dramatic mountain backdrops against which to build power dams or launch glitzy political campaigns — it also carries a long reputation for bigotry and ideological excess. The Dunsmuir coalmines had a reputation throughout western Canada for exploitation of Chinese labour (paid at half the daily rate of white workers), unsafe working conditions, and for resisting unionization. Among the preoccupations of James Dunsmuir's government were ways of limiting oriental immigration. Public suspicion of undue personal enrichment has attached itself to many of its entrepreneurial premiers, from Dunsmuir and his building of the Esquimalt and Nanaimo Railway, to Bill Bennett and Vander Zalm in recent times. W.A.C. Bennett's government brought in anti-labor legislation, kept strict limits on social welfare programmes, and customarily campaigned for re-election on the basis of "Red Tide" characterizations of its CCF and NDP opposition. Vancouver was the site in 1914 of the turning away of the *Komagata Maru*, a ship loaded with 376 would-be immigrants from India, most of them veterans of the British army and thereby legally entitled to entry to Canada. In 1942, it was anti-Japanese hysteria among British Columbians that prompted the Canadian government to intern even Canadian-born Japanese-Canadians under the War Measures Act.

In joining Bill Bennett's Social Credit party in the mid-1980s, Kim Campbell may have been pragmatically attaching herself to a party that could give her access to power, but she was also attaching herself to the party's twenty-five-year history of carrying out British Columbia's penchant for a polarized, anti-labour, entrepreneurial government. By doing so she was also repeating the preference she had shown a decade earlier in her marriage to Nathan Divinsky, whom Campbell friends interviewed by the *Star*'s Judy Steed consistently characterized in terms of "Thatcher-Reagan" politics. "Very reactionary and elitist," one described him ("with affection") to Steed. "A neo-conservative before it became fashionable," said another, "... a guy who stood against the collective."

The evolving effect of Campbell's association with the Social Credit dynasty in B.C. has been nearly as bizarre as many of the political episodes in that province. Her choosing to associate with it, and her ultimate breaking with it, have both worked to her advantage. Although her role with Social Credit was a minor one — an unelected executive director of Premier Bill Bennett's office in 1985-86, and a backbench MLA under the Vander Zalm government for the riding of Vancouver-Point Grey in 1986-88 — its significance in her public biography has continued to grow. As *Alberta Report* has noted, her bid for the Social Credit leadership, in which she received only fourteen of some 1,100 votes, finishing last among twelve candidates, was taken seriously by neither the party nor the media. The speech in which she delivered her now famous characterization of Vander Zalm — "Charisma without substance is a dangerous thing" (translated by *L'actualité* earlier this year as "une belle tête avec rien dedans, cela peut être dangereux" — a translation which itself contributes to a process of exaggeration and mythologizing) — was virtually unreported by local or national media. Over the years, however, as her career in federal politics has advanced, her Socred leadership bid has slowly taken on legendary size. It has come not only to link her to the high-profile and dramatic rightist politics of the Socred succession (and thus to *magnify* her by appearing to insert her into that succession), but it has also more and more come to characterize her as the person who tried bravely and vainly to save that succession from failure and corruption. The line "Charisma without substance" has grown in the Canadian consciousness from a scarcely registered scrap of campaign rhetoric to a prescient pronouncement of right-wing doom. Once the naïve fool of the B.C. Socred conservatism, Kim Campbell has become now at very least its Cassandra.

At the same time, her very public break with Vander Zalm and his anti-abortion policies, together with her later gun control legislation and attempt to legislate a limited set of rights for homosexuals, have gained her — among many feminists, Red Tories, and "small-l" liberals unlikely ever to vote Conservative — the reputation of being the best of a bad lot. The Social Crediters of Bennett and Vander Zalm may not have been a sensitive and caring group, but they most certainly provided an ideal background against which a right-leaning politician could appear to be courageously sensitive and caring. The dramatic effect of the contrast between this background and Campbell's March 1988 decision to defy it can be seen in the headline images of her that immediately followed:

> Free Speaker: Kim Campbell's political rise is marked by moves like breaking Socred ranks over abortion. (*Vancouver Magazine*, April 1988)
>
> Fiery Campbell launched as Tory. (*The Vancouver Sun*, 19 October 1988)
>
> Renegade leading the charge. (*The Globe and Mail*, 25 October 1988)
>
> Brash new Tory heading east. (*The Globe and Mail*, 24 November 1988)
>
> Passionate pro-choicer named justice minister. (*The Globe and Mail*, 24 February 1990)

> Vancouver MP is 1st woman justice minister: Campbell has earned reputation for willingness to speak her mind. (*The Montreal Gazette*, 24 February 1990)
>
> Candid Kim: success no fluke. (*The Vancouver Sun*, 24 February 1990)

After her three-year association with Social Credit, Campbell's image now presents itself magically transformed — from a Bill Bennett acolyte to a "passionate," "brash," free-speaking leader of 'progressive' causes. In the rhetorical enthusiasm of the headlines, the magic itself appears to promise new wonders.

■

> Campbell and Divinsky were founding investors in Bridges, which survived the vicissitudes of the restaurant trade over the last decade to become one of Vancouver's established dining spots. I was taken there by Fritz and Shirley Bowers, old friends of Campbell and Divinsky. We drank white wine and gazed out at a lowering gray sky, listening to clanking sailboats moored at False Creek marina on Granville Island. Beyond the masts loomed the Vancouver skyline and the mountains.
>
> Fritz and Shirley (his third wife; they are a much married group, these Vancouverites) still get together with Tuzie [Divinsky] (and his third wife) once a month for gourmet feasts. (Judy Steed, *The Toronto Star*)

Throughout the spring of 1993 political commentators have followed Campbell's lead in associating her name with British Columbia scenery, geography, wealth, and lifestyle. To some extent the entire public presentation of "Campbell" has resembled a lifestyle advertisement, a photo-op against snow-capped mountains. British Columbia is presented as a leisure society, where businesses outlast recessions, restaurants have sea and mountain views, and diners have time to drink a wine course before their meals and to gaze absent-mindedly at sky, masts, skyline, and mountains. There is little urgency. The sailboats are moored, the sky changes slowly, new marriage partners are easily available (unlike in Ottawa, where Campbell was reported to have candidly confessed last fall to a convention of 400 woman journalists to have found life in federal politics "sometimes unspeakable lonely" [Newman 52, Riley 13-14]). The boating image is repeated later in Steed's article in a note that Campbell lived with her second husband "in a houseboat," and in Vastel's *L'actualité* comment that with her second husband she "would have been able to lead a life of perfect love on his 15 m. boat, anchored at the Sidney marina, on Vancouver Island."

Quebec commentators have been particularly enamoured of this equation of Campbell with B.C. images of prosperity and leisure. For Vastel, in an amusing pun on Quebec Catholicism, B.C. geography, and the bare skin of Barbara Woodley's photograph, "Campbell" is "La Madonna de Port Alberni." In mid-April of this year, *La Presse* ran a four-part series on the culture, geography, and current politics of British Columbia; although none of the four articles dealt even peripherally with Campbell or with issues raised by her campaign, the series was titled "Au pays de Kim Campbell."

Quebec's strong interest in both British Columbia and Campbell — Québécois columnists Lysiane Gagnon (*La Presse*) and Pauline Couture (*The Globe and Mail*) were the first to announce the occurrence of "Campbellmania" — probably rests in part on Campbell's *not* being from a province normally viewed in Quebec culture as indifferent or antagonistic to francophone interests, on her not being from Ontario, Newfoundland, or Manitoba. It rests, it would seem, also on British Columbia being the most distant, exotic, and unknown anglophone province for the Québécois. But it rests in addition, I suggest, on Quebec's own history and mythology. In reading francophone novels set in western Canada, including Georges Bugnet's *Nypsa* and Gabriele Roy's *La Route d'Altamont*, E.D. Blodgett has noted how the image of the *voyageur* persists in Canadian francophone literature either as a nostalgic recollection or as a "travel" metaphor for a young francophone's personal development. He argues that the "closing" of the Old West to francophones, with the Canadian government's purchase of the Hudson Bay Company lands in 1870 and the transformation of the Company's British Columbia lands into a crown colony in 1858, was as nearly significant psychologically to Quebec culture as was Wolfe's defeat of the French army in 1759.

Indeed, before 1759, the frontiers of New France ranged effectively far past Ontario and the Mississippi basin, through the Saskatchewan River systems to the Rocky Mountain foothills. While British fur traders tended to establish bases in which to await the arrival of Indians eager to sell furs, the French, following adventurers like La Salle and La Vérendrye, ranged far into the hinterland in annual fur-purchasing ventures. After 1759, the continental fur trade consolidated in Montreal, with Québécois voyageurs continuing to provide most of its workforce. The crews of the North-West Company's overland explorers — like Alexander Mackenzie, who traveled from Lake Athabaska to the Mackenzie River delta in 1789 and to the British Columbia coast near Bella Coola in 1793, and Simon Fraser, who reached the mouth of the Fraser River in 1808 — were nearly all French-speaking Métis and Québécois. Our own times remember the

English-speaking "heroes" Mackenzie and Fraser, but forget Mackenzie's five voyageurs and Fraser's nineteen. They forget also that the working language of many of the forts of the fur trade in British Columbia, as late as the 1850s, was French. This extension of Quebec culture into British Columbia is evidenced today by a scattering of place names along the old canoe routes: Pouce Coupé, Cache Creek, Quesnel, Lac la Hache, Babine Lake, Francois Lake, Miette Pass, Ne-Parle-Pas Rapids, Porte d'Enfer (Hell's Gate Canyon).

This double revision of Quebec's psychological frontiers, back from New Orleans and back from the Pacific coast, has been less the "closing" that Blodgett proposes than a pushing back into the heart of modern Quebec itself. The psychological frontiers of most twentieth-century Québécois writing have been internal — within Montreal, within the culture, within families, within the self-tortured minds of the characters. English-Canadian scenes and symbols, from any part of the country, rarely appear in this fiction except as a source of oppression. The few exceptions to this intensely focused fiction have usually not involved ventures into English-Canada or into the world at large as much as they have symbolic journeys that implicitly re-create the adventures of seventeenth- and eighteenth-century French explorers. Here, once outside Quebec, the world becomes exotic rather than realistic: the orient of Jean Basile's *Les Voyages d'Irkoutsk* or *La Jument des Mongols*; the arctic of Yves Thériault's *Agaguk*, *Tayaout*, and *Agoak*; the south Pacific of Victor-Lévy Beaulieu's epic *Monsieur Melville*; the California of his *Jack Kerouac* or Jacques Poulin's *Volkswagen Blues*; or the seductive Vancouver of Pierre Nepveu's *L'hiver de Mira Christophe*. In Beaulieu's *Monsieur Melville* the narrator's urge to break out of his feelings of entrapment is displaced onto the celebrated south sea voyages of James Cook,

Antoine de Bougainville, and the Compte de la Pérouse, from which only Bougainville returned alive. In *Volkswagen Blues*, the characters, searching for a missing brother, literally follow the route of early explorers to California. "They had set out from Gaspé, where Jacques Cartier discovered Canada, and followed the St. Lawrence and the Great Lakes, then the old Mississippi, Father of the Waters, right to St. Louis, and then taken the Oregon Trail in the footsteps of the emigrants of the nineteenth century who had formed caravans and set out in search of the lost Paradise with their oxen-drawn chariots." At the end of the voyageur routes in Nepveu's *L'hiver de Mira Christophe* is a confusingly paradisal Vancouver that alters personalities and dreams. It is this lost and ambiguous Paradise that one can see today flickering in Quebec idealizations of both "Kim Campbell" and "British Columbia."

The exotic, of course, as several critics have commented about Thériault's portrayals of the Inuit, is often built on ignorance. Not a great deal of information about English-Canada reaches francophone Quebec, nor is there usually much desire there for it. Michel Vastel laments the public idealization of Kim Campbell, complaining that unseen is "a reality more ... prosaic," but his article is accompanied by a full-page colour photo of a pixie-like Campbell posing with another sign of Vancouver, an open umbrella. In a sense, this photo returns us to the one with which we began. A smiling gaze into the camera. A solo act with one very large prop. No one else in the picture. Lots of empty space for fantasy, in any official language.

NOTE:
PERMISSION TO USE THIS
WELL-KNOWN PHOTOGRAPH OF
KIM CAMPBELL BARE-SHOULDERED,
HOLDING LEGAL ROBES, WAS REFUSED FIRST
BY KIM CAMPBELL'S ASSISTANT AND
SUBSEQUENTLY BY BARBARA WOODLEY.

READERS MAY WISH TO CLIP A REPRODUCTION
OF IT FROM A NEWSPAPER OR MAGAZINE OF
THEIR CHOICE AND AFFIX IT TO THIS SPACE.

CHAPTER IV

The Sexual Body

> Chez les femmes, c'est la favorite dans la course à la direction du parti conservateur, la ministre de la Défense Kim Campbell, qui est jugée la plus sexy des élues qui fréquentent la colline parlementaire. (*La Presse*, 1 May, 1993: G1)

Barbara Woodley's celebrated photo of Kim Campbell, first published in her book *Portraits: Canadian Women in Focus*, raises a large number of questions and issues, including one that has tugged at me from time to time during the preceding chapters: why am I writing this book? The photo, taken during the apparent privacy of changing clothes, places all who see it in the position of voyeurs who look at the woman and the photo as "objects" of both desire and aesthetic satisfaction. For male viewers, for whom this is a customary, culturally entrenched way to regard, or "gaze" at a woman, this position of voyeur is almost overwhelming. Vastel, for example, comments sardonically at the speed with which British tabloids inserted the photo among their arrays of bare-breasted shop-girls and starlets, but cannot himself resist naming her an English-Canadian "Madonna." In miniature, the photo catches the male, and even the lesbian, viewer staring at the bare-shouldered and potentially nude Campbell with the same sort of self-interested fascination as this book has in gazing at the multiplicity of "Campbell" images — delighting in contradiction and irony, alert for the concealed, admiring and mistrusting, grateful for what has been offered, but fearful that there will be nothing else. Fearful even that the legal robes that Campbell's right hand raises toward the camera predict a series of legalistic refusals. Might her government plead that it has economic "headaches"? Might it offer no affectionate social programmes? Might there be no warm, soft skin, only the black, flat surface of the Law?

This gaze, popularly viewed as one of "love/hate," and in its extreme forms re-enacted daily on the crime pages of our newspapers, is enormously problematical. And this problem exists not just in Canada but throughout western culture: the woman is seen as promising (by being beautiful, by being charming) to give and, simultaneously, as hypocritically not giving. She is the "cock-teaser," the rape victim who, because of her attractive body or attractive dress, was believed by her attacker to have been "asking for it."

For myself, who am known to have written extensively about Canadian women writers — Audrey Thomas, Margaret Atwood, Daphne Marlatt in particular — the Woodley photo confronts me with a serious problem in undertaking my own "look" at "Kim Campbell." Do I, when I am attracted to write about the books these women have written and then suggest problems or gaps within them, in a sense "beat up" the women, much as violent husbands in our culture batter the wives who have disappointed them? When I emphasize the things which these books do not do, or emphasize the policies that Kim Campbell's public image appears not to promise, am I becoming one of those violent, disappointed men? Am I punishing, through my criticism of these particular women, all of the women who have smiled at me but not loved me, or the women who have loved me but only in an adult way — *on condition*? And who have remained capable of raising those conditions, as Campbell raises the robes of legal condition between us and her smooth-skinned body here? Why is it, one might well ask, that it is "Kim Campbell" that I write my first general-audience political book about, and not a male politician?

I don't have strong answers to these questions, except to suggest that for men to depend on the history of male abuse of women to avoid interacting with them socially, politically, or philosophically, is also potentially abusive. Men can be expected to disagree with women on issues of politics or literature, much as women frequently disagree on these with both women and men, and as men themselves disagree with other men. Particularly because Kim Campbell has proposed herself a leader for both men and women — has put herself up for viewing, so to speak — both sexes need to look seriously, however difficult or psychologically complicated that may be, at the "Kim Campbell" she presents. Can I look at this woman without seeing her as men historically have tended to see women? Probably not, since I inevitably live, like all of us, *inside* the cultural conventions that continue, in Canada and in the rest of the western world, to portray man as viewer, and woman, as in the Woodley photo, as a visually beautiful promise.

What I can do, however, is work to weaken the force of such conventions by identifying them, to myself, and to readers who may find it useful to note their operation, whether in this book or in the perception of "Kim Campbell" elsewhere. I can point out, as I will in a later chapter, how this cultural tradition in which men act and gaze, and women wait to be gazed upon, creates special difficulties for a woman like Campbell when she seeks power within political structures created by men. I can also point out that, at least consciously, I write this book as much more than just a man gazing at the image of an attractive woman. I write as a person born, like Campbell, in British Columbia, of a parent whose family extends back into the United Empire Loyalist period. I write as someone with a direct interest in Canadian culture, in the survival of the Canadian nation — as a writer whose books are read mainly because they are "Canadian," as a teacher of Canadian literature and culture who might have little to do should the nation fail. I write also as a Canadian who benefits from the prosperity and cultural morale of other Canadians. When unemployment, business failure, school overcrowding, hospital underfunding, or slowdowns in artistic and cultural activity occur, the environment of every one of us is impoverished. It is our children, our friends, the friends of our friends who are unemployed or unable to attend school; our streets that are pocked with empty storefronts; our libraries and bookstores that have fewer wonderful Canadian books; our museums that will have less art. We all have a lot riding on the inviting shoulders of "Kim Campbell." I say. And then I return, uneasily, to staring at Woodley's photo.

■

There have not been very many such photos of Canadian politicians. Until the photos of Pierre Trudeau performing jackknife dives from a high board, most photographs showed the Canadian politician solemnly attired, as if dressing for politics were similar to dressing for church. The Trudeau photographs relaxed this image, but they also drew attention to his athleticism and vigour. They portrayed him as a profoundly active man, the grandstanding athlete, presented him within an active/passive model of male-female relations similar to that implied, in a very different way, by the waiting, looked-upon Campbell of the Woodley photo. Responding to and completing this image, young girls screamed at his arrivals during the 1968 federal election campaign, and clamoured for his touch or kiss, much as if he were a similarly active and "performing" male rock star. Campbell has to date done little in the way of "dramatic" gestures to counter the visual portrayal of her as quiet and waiting. As the *Globe*'s Ross Howard notes, "no pirouettes, piano demonstrations or plunges into crowds with false bonhomie for this candidate."

The only Canadian male politician to pose for a photograph that invited the kind of active gaze normally solicited by a photo of a woman has been Peter Kormos, a minister in the Ontario cabinet of Bob Rae. Kormos posed as a "Sunshine Boy" for the tabloid *Toronto Sun*. The publication of his photo prompted a storm of protest that it implicitly sanctioned the portrayal of both men and women as sex-objects, and resulted in his dismissal from the cabinet. The major differences between his photograph and Woodley's of Campbell are those of class and audience. His photograph appeared in a right-of-centre tabloid read mostly by working-class readers. The format of its presentation was similar to that of the paper's "Sunshine Girl," a feature it frequently captions with crude sexual innuendo. In contrast, Campbell's photo appeared first in a tastefully decorated Ottawa art gallery, in the company of photographs of implicitly feminist women. Later it appeared in a coffee-table book that collected these photos. The audience of Kormos' photo was emphatically heterosexual; the Sunshine Boy feature is run in the *Sun* as a way of balancing sexual treatment, of offering female readers the same "treats" the Sunshine Girl offers male readers. The implied audience of the Woodley photo exhibition and book was mostly female. The photos were presented as a celebration of women and women's accomplishments, presented by a woman and for women. In fact, the people who protested Kormos' posing for the *Sun* seem to have been a significant part of the intended audience of Woodley's exhibition.

Twentieth-century art history has made most of us aware of how a change in context can change the meaning and status of an object. A discarded urinal picked up and signed, pseudonymously, by artist Marcel Duchamp, titled *Fountain*, and ushered by him otherwise unchanged through the doors of an art gallery, ultimately became a prized high-art "sculpture" within France's national collection. To an extent, the reverse has happened to Woodley's photo of Campbell: its being taken out of the gallery, and out of the pages of Woodley's book of photos, and inserted into the pages of newspapers, where it then rubbed its bare shoulders with Campbell's political duties as minister of justice, changed its audience and changed its status. It was no longer merely a classy photo of a classy woman. It was now also — like the photo of Kormos — an anomaly among political images. Ultimately, irony of ironies, it would be published in the same context as that of the Kormos photo — in British tabloids that depend, like the *Sun*, on sensational photos and stories to maintain working-class readerships.

This change in context also placed Woodley's Kim Campbell photo beside another curious set of political images — that of the publicly beautiful or publicly seductive woman who parlays her having been "looked-upon" into political action. The Italian hard-core pornography actress "Cicciolina" (Ilona Stall) successfully runs for her country's parliament. Brigitte Bardot becomes a powerful animal-rights activist. Jane Fonda becomes the anti-Vietnam War activist "Hanoi Jane." Anita Bryant campaigns against homosexuality. The public beauty here seems to work paradoxically to make the political views of the woman appear legitimate. The passive, looked-upon aspect of the woman — her "REAL-womanness," we might say — allows her also to possess action and credibility.

Media response to this major shift in the context of the Woodley photo from art gallery to tabloid — surprise, delight, amusement, excitement — suggests that the shift did Kim Campbell the politician much more good than harm. All of the original meanings and associations of the photo — a classy woman, a feminist success — have remained in play. By remaining in play, they have framed and qualified the new meanings — pin-up girl, Sunshine Girl, sexual woman — allowing these to operate not as contradictions but as interesting additions to the original meanings. These meanings in turn have allowed many more people to "look" at the photo. The original female and art audience is now supplemented by a much larger audience of both sexes who see not "art," but "not-your-usual-photo-of-a-politician." For some, as in the cases of Bardot or Fonda, the attractiveness of the image even adds to Campbell's political credibility. Moreover, the unusual photo that the new larger audience sees is also very much an "OK" photo — no Peter Kormos scandal here — for it has been declared "OK" by its previous high-class history as "Real Art."

■

But there is still much more in this image of bare shoulders, slight smile, robes on a hanger than simply an unusual or provocative photo, or the photo itself would not continue to be reprinted and talked about. It is a powerful photo not only in the usual way of such photos — in what it conceals, and in what it displays by concealing — but also in what it uses to conceal.

Despite the high contrast it presents between the uncovered, uninterpreted female body and the formality and "heavy" meaning of the legal robes, the photo is remarkably peaceful and reassuring. The woman's face, with its faint and patient smile, expresses no strong emotion. There is an immediate comparison activated here between Campbell's image and various conventions in our culture of the portrayal of women in the nude. The portrayal we are perhaps most familiar with is the vamp, the *Playboy* centrefold who presents her body boldly saying, in effect, "Here I am, and are you, big boy, really up to dealing with me?" The second most familiar portrayal is that of comic surprise, the woman unexpectedly intruded upon in bath or shower, standing knees together, arms crossed across her breasts, face at least pretending shock and outrage. While this portrayal still appears frequently on television, in the movies of the past two decades it has been largely replaced by a third presentation: woman as lover, filmed unselfconsciously naked with a partner. A fourth portrayal. however, the unclothed woman viewed unawares at bath or in bed, is the one that appears most often in post-Renaissance painting. All of these portrayals carry a strong sexual charge. The vamp appears to invite intercourse, and to welcome the camera's lens. The surprised woman appears to fear both; her crossed arms and locked knees suggest that for her the intrusion of the lens into her privacy threatens unwelcome penetration. The woman filmed unselfconsciously with her partner has accepted sexual activity, and has also ostensibly accepted its documentation by the camera. The woman painted unawares is in perhaps the most ostensibly perilous situation. The painter's intrusion is not an accident, as it is usually made to appear in the case of the surprised woman. The painter has *chosen* to intrude, and appears to be seizing the image of the woman's body without her agreement.

Of these four conventions, it is the surprised woman that the Woodley photo most resembles. But the surprise is mild. The woman did not plan on being viewed this way — the robes she holds before her tell us this — but she is neither alarmed nor horrified. Sexual relations here are not a large issue — they are not invited, not feared, not implied as being even subliminally on the mind of the "painter" or photographer. With the slight smile, the woman acknowledges herself as a sexual being, but *that*, she suggests, is for another context, or other people. In political terms, this is a powerful, reassuring, and humanizing image. This woman is not troubled by her sexuality, the image tells us; sexuality does not disrupt her friendships, her daily business, or her own peace of mind. Even more important in a politician, this woman responds well to surprises. If we burst in on her while she is dressing, she will most likely respond, as here, with grace, poise, and calm.

Moreover, the photo implies that if we burst in on her while she is without clothing, the law — regulation, convention, order — will still be in place, protecting all of us. It is, after all, legal robes she holds with her right hand between us and her body, enforcing decorum and due process. If we are going to encounter this woman's body, it will be in the "right" way. The robes do not so much bar the way as they ensure correct, regulated passage. In this scene, the clothes both do and do not make the woman. Even if apparently nude, her body remains qualified by law, and offers an emblem to those women who also would wish to present their bodies as sexual bodies, but would do so in safety. In fact, the legal robes here become physical symbols of the amended "rape-shield" provisions of the Criminal Code, which Campbell was instrumental in getting passed in June of 1992. Behind them, Campbell's body becomes the body of all women, calmly protected by the law which her right hand holds in front of both the prying eyes of the camera and the prying questions of the accused rapist's attorney. Hovering over the entire photo is our culture's image of justice, a blindfolded woman, holding out a set of scales that protects us. But our photo's justice is watchful rather than blindfolded; its law remains balanced — on the hanger, and on the woman's fingers — and also clear-cut — the "black and white" of robe and collar.

Even male viewers, voyeuristic as we may be, can find reassurance in this "rape-shield" image. If we observe the law as well as gaze at the woman, we are told, nothing will go wrong. The law is a barrier, but not a rigid or inflexible one, to the desired body beyond. The patient smile offers that guarantee. If the man observes the law, at some distant moment access will be granted. In exchange, there will be no awkward misunderstandings, no recriminations, no scenes of sobbing or shouting, no surprise charges of assault or rape. The robes, then, guarantee not only the safety of the particular woman and of women in general; they also appear to guarantee harmonious sexual exchange. There can be embrace and exchange. When it occurs it will be sanctioned, covered, abetted by the law. It will be, in the ultimate sense, "safe sex." Again there are vague metaphors present here about future social policy under a Campbell government. The response of "Kim Campbell" to her fellow citizens will be legalistic, the image hints, but not entirely uncaring. The warm skin of a gentle social policy may be well regulated, but it will still be there, and be there because of the law.

And this is not all. As I naughtily continue to stare at this picture, yet more meanings appear, stemming again from the various forms the presentation of nude women has taken in our culture — the vamp, the surprised girl, the lover, and the relaxing woman, surreptitiously viewed. This "Kim Campbell" is so much not these women. Surrounded by gauze curtains, her hair and make-up discretely done, her gaze back at us untroubled, her hand firmly on the law, this woman is above all more sophisticated than any of those four. She is in unhurried control, confident not only of her sexuality and her relation to law but also of her standing in the world. No element in her image is strained or exaggerated. Here in abundance is what the sophisticated woman is rumoured to promise: savoir faire, no hang-ups (except for the clothes which are themselves not to get messed on the floor), a good upbringing, no childhood traumas, no incest, bestiality, dirty laundry, malnutrition, future health problems. To accept this woman — as either woman or prime minister — is to take, the photo is telling me, very little risk. Here is no *Pygmalion/My Fair Lady* story of a poor urchin, re-educated. Here is no woman of uncertain breeding, who may in the future develop any number of bizarre problems because of casual nutrition, or unsupervised hours in front of Saturday cartoons. This woman has a reliable history of "class."

This latter aspect of the photo fits neatly with other "Kim Campbell" mythologies, particularly with the story of her making herself anew when only twelve years old. She may have had a troubled childhood, but she erased this with her own classy efforts. Became the first female president of her high school student council. Her graduating class's valedictorian. Worked her way through college while serving on its student council. Won admission to a prestigious graduate school.

■

Kim Campbell, Kim Campbell, je veux bien, mais avez-vous pensé, avant de vous jeter dans ses bras, aux boulets qu'elle tire avec elle? Spécialement au Québec? Spécialement à Laval? Pour les beaux yeux de Kim, vous réélirez Della Noce? (Pierre Foglia, *La Presse*, 15 April 1993)

Pierre Foglia's characterization of Kim Campbell as someone with "beautiful eyes," and with arms into which one might wish to throw oneself, even at the expense of re-electing an undesirable Tory incumbent, demonstrates the extent to which the construction of woman as desirable object continues to influence the way in which Campbell is perceived. A general ambience of sexuality surrounds "Kim Campbell," much in excess of that which surrounds the images of other female politicians. This ambience is not the product of one bare-shouldered photograph, but rather the result of a combination of factors about which the photo appears to have focused awareness. Many of these factors come from her term as minister of justice when, like Pierre Trudeau before her, "Campbell" became associated in the public mind with issues of sexuality and sexual conduct. Trudeau announced that the nation had no business in the nation's bedrooms, and by saying so inadvertently made his own bedroom seem more interesting than before. Campbell, in a series of public policy positions in which she repeatedly risked her career, affirmed the sexual control of women over their own bodies. Although other women politicians were taking similar positions, the fact that Campbell as a Social Credit or Conservative politician, a rare woman among right-wing men, was indeed *risking* her career — in a sense laying her body on the line in a way similar to that in which Canadian women place their bodies at risk in their everyday interactions with men — sexualized both her image and her perceived relationship to her male colleagues.

Campbell's first appearance in the national media, in fact, came on an issue of women's sexuality and reproductive freedom, when she broke with the Vander Zalm cabinet over its plans to cease the funding of clinical abortion. The pro-choice position, that Campbell appeared to affirm here, the position that women should be able to choose whether or not to terminate a pregnancy, also implicitly contains a pro-sexuality position. Women, it implies, and even very young women, should also be able to decide whether or not to be sexually active. They should have the freedom to enjoy sexual relations without paying a "penalty" of childbirth, and the freedom to refuse sexual invasion by aborting a foetus conceived through rape.

While she was minister of justice, Campbell's policies continued to associate her with issues and decisions that raised images of consensual sexual intercourse. One of her first actions in 1990 was to introduce Bill C-43, a bill that re-introduced abortion to the Criminal Code but in a way that legalized many more abortion options than had earlier Criminal Code provisions. When this bill failed to receive Senate approval, it was her ministry that permitted the current situation — in which women and doctors are free from Criminal Code regulation of abortion decisions — to continue as de facto policy. And she herself as minister declared herself "pro-choice," and therefore "quite comfortable without legislation" (*Alberta Report*).

In 1991, she introduced gun-control legislation that was correctly perceived by the public as a direct response to the Montreal "massacre" of fourteen female engineering students by Marc Lepine in 1989. Although the sexual overtones of this legislation were less explicit, they were nevertheless strong. Lepine's phallic gun had violated the bodies of the fourteen women. The violation was widely perceived to be a "systemic" one: Lepine had enacted the fantasy violence of countless other disaffected Canadian men toward women. It was the young women's independence, their apparent "freedom," that had enraged Lepine.

He regarded their independence as excessive and undeserved, as allowing them to undertake engineering careers while he felt he was denied such independence and choice. He killed them because he perceived them to be "feminists." Campbell's legislation appeared directed toward preserving this feminism, to limiting the phallic authority of anti-feminist, gun-bearing males. It was opposed, somewhat on gender lines, within the Tory caucus. Right-wing male MPs, many from rural constituencies, and many who had opposed the legalization of abortion, opposed the bill as an infringement of basic "rights." They opposed also the legislation's premise that the Lepine misogyny was a systemic misogyny, that guns in Canada represented a general threat to the lives and freedoms of women. Although many feminists have lamented the compromise bill that Campbell eventually succeeded in getting passed into law, the fact that Campbell appeared to battle for the legislation, and succeeded in at least circumcising some Canadian guns — limiting the size of magazines, forbidding the sale of specific weapons — again portrayed her to the general public as a defender of gender freedom.

Campbell's work during 1991-92 with the "rape-shield" provisions of the Criminal Code — provisions to protect complainants from undue inquiry by the defendant into their sexual history, and to shift the burden of proving whether or not sexual consent had been given from complainant to defendant — again associated her strongly with images of genitalia and intercourse. Consensual sex was here to be distinguished and defended from coerced and violently achieved sexual exploitation of a human body. The provisions regarding the complainant's sexual history were particularly significant for Campbell's image. The complainant, the legislation implied, had a right to a sexual history. She did not have to be a virgin, or of "previously unblemished character"; the very notion of "blemish" was radically challenged. Sexually active unmarried women had the right to the protection of the law's legal robes.

In 1992-93, Campbell's proposal, in Bill C-108, to amend the Human Rights Act in order to protect the rights of homosexuals further extended this image of a liberal and generous understanding of human sexuality. Although the legislation was not her personal initiative, done as it was in response to a court ruling, she was again attacked by far-right members of the Tory caucus, and by ultra-conservative sectors of the media, for encouraging decadence and sacrificing moral values. Meanwhile the half-measures of the legislation — it would not institutionalize same-sex marriages — and her own failure to fight strongly enough for the bill to win it caucus support, earned her the hostility of the gay community. The net effect of the controversy, however, within a generally heterosexual Canadian culture, was to affirm the image of a pro-sexuality "Kim Campbell."

■

A political scientist and lawyer by training, she once admitted "I'm a sucker for intelligent men." She has twice married men several years her senior and is twice divorced. (*Alberta Report*)

SUDBURY (CP) — This year's Miss Elliot Lake pageant has become the latest beauty contest to be cancelled after Lori Richer, an unwed mother, tried to become a contestant. Richer, 18, wanted to enter the pageant against the wishes of Debbie Furoy, the event's chairperson.

When Richer refused to relinquish her quest for the crown, Furoy recommended to the Uranium Festival

> Committee, chaired by Mayor George Faroukh, that the contest be called off.
>
> Organizers blamed the decision on soaring costs, but the flagship pageant had been under fire for its elegibility rules. It was open only to women who had never been married, never lived common-law and had no children. (*The Toronto Star,* 9 May 1993)

A number of journalists have commented, directly or obliquely, on the known facts of Campbell's marital history and their presumed relevance or irrelevance to her political standing. In the quotation above, *Alberta Report* slyly juxtaposes her professional training with her marriage record, implying that her failures in marriage diminish her credibility as a political scientist and lawyer. Lawyers, it suggests, should not be "suckers" in love. Two thousand miles east, in the pages of *L'actualité,* Michel Vastel suggests that the current fashion of "la *political correctness*" has prevented the media from asking "certain questions with too much frankness," but goes on himself to report that some journalists have been looking into "the 'painful' circumstances of Mme. Campbell's second divorce," and that "allusions to the relationship between the future prime minister and her former deputy minister of Justice, John Tait," may be only days away. In *The Toronto Star,* Rosemary Speirs speculates openly on why Campbell's "sex, style and divorces don't appear to be issues" in her leadership campaign, and goes on to quote pollster Donna Dasko as saying "What I find amazing about Kim Campbell's candidacy is that there has been so little negative comment about her gender and the facts of her life. Her status is not an asset to her, but it does not appear to be a negative factor. So far it looks like a neutral factor."

My own sense, based on the public profile of Campbell's record as minister of justice, and on her dramatic rise to national prominence through her rupture with B.C. Social Credit, is that "the facts of her life" have become a peculiar asset. "Kim Campbell" has in a way become a symbol of the way most men and women encounter gender relations. Optimistic and well-meaning, they rush into relationships that become at some point disappointing, painful, or, as in Lori Richer's case, personally restricting. At worst, they require surgical or legal intervention — the shelter of the legal robes an experienced but still hopeful image holds up in the Barbara Woodley photo. In a sense, the female body of "Kim Campbell" reminds us that if she is denied opportunity, like Richer, because of her sexuality, any of us can also be restricted because of ours. There is no evidence that the Campbell campaign understands the power of this image, or has taken any steps to exploit it. But there is evidence that the media, subliminally at least, have understood. Here Campbell's rivals — the male competitors for the Tory leadership, the leaders of the other parties — are presented mostly in head-and-shoulders images. Campbell, however, is presented in historical shots from her youth and childhood — playing guitar, sitting on Santa's knee, delivering the valedictory address at Prince of Wales High School, or in similar full-length shots in the present. It is her female body, a body that includes its ongoing sexual history, that is presented here — that is offered, as in Woodley's "Kim Campbell", for approbation and embrace.

Photo: Canapress

CHAPTER V

The Anglo Speaks French

> The director of the École Alexandra looked at my name and welcomed us with open arms. Then she heard me pronounce my name and frowned. This was not a school for anglophones, she said, particularly in the higher grades. We brought out the children's immersion credentials and everyone smiled again. (Peter Desbarats)

In 1988 when I moved to Paris and began a one-year's stay in France, one of my biggest surprises occurred when I began to watch French television regularly. I discovered that in France the language of romance and cultural magic was English. Whereas in many American and English-Canadian TV commercials for cosmetics or wine the ultimate phrases used to "prove" the value of a product are a few words of French, or French-accented English — "Eet's got — how you say — zee hedge?" — murmured by one lover into the forgiving ear of another, on French TV the power of a shampoo or the stylishness of an automobile was demonstrated by lovers who responded in a few quaint words of English. In Quebec's French-language television of the same period, one was unlikely to hear English at all, except satirical or farcical lines in situation comedies. And at hockey or baseball games in Toronto or Vancouver, a singer who ventured even part of the national anthem in French might have been emphatically booed.

What it means to speak French or English in Canada is an extremely variable and complex thing. Mispronounce your own name, at least by the standards of one of the languages, as Peter Desbarats reports doing above, and you may jeopardize the education of your children. Speak English in the wrong Quebec context — as my small son did loudly one sleepless night in 1975, in a solidly francophone campground beside an amphibian-filled lake, calling out "Why won't those frogs stop talking?" — and you create at very least profound embarrassment. In the Canadian tradition of accidental bilingualism, the Laurentian campground was prophetically named "Le Camping Bou-Bou."

One of the major misconceptions in Canadian culture involves the way in which we have defined ourselves as a "bilingual" country. As the Official Languages Act of 1969 and the Charter of Rights and Freedoms of 1982 both make clear, Canadians have, through their elected representatives, defined themselves not as individually bilingual, or even as culturally bilingual, but as institutionally bilingual. We have created no guarantees that we will hear both English and French spoken in all parts of the country. We have not pledged to learn to speak both languages, or to train our children in both languages. We have not in any active sense attempted to "shove" French or English, as the quintessentially English-Canadian expression delicately phrases it, down any of our own throats. We have only pledged to make federal government services available in both official languages to all citizens in all parts of country and, under the Charter, minority official-language education available wherever the size of the minority language community warrants.

The effects of Canada's official language policies have

been both complex and awkward. Institutional bilingualism, by creating an equality of status for French and English in Parliament, in federal departments, agencies, and crown corporations, spreads both languages to all parts of the country in a proportion usually quite unrepresentative of the actual languages spoken in any given region. Canadians encounter both equally in their national parks, on their currency, on the federally regulated labels of consumer products, but in their daily lives often encounter no one who speaks the "other" official language for months at a time. The perception that bilingualism is an asset in Canada in gaining professional employment, particularly employment within the federal civil service or with federal agencies has, however, motivated many English-Canadians to demand French-language education for their children. This demand has led many provinces, and local school boards, to expand French-language education, introducing it in lower grades than before, and offering in many cases choices among partial immersion, full immersion, and single-course programs. Even in western Canada, where resistance to throat-shoved bilingualism has been legendary, parents have been known to line up in the dark hours of the morning in order to enroll their children in French immersion schools.

Thus, although institutional bilingualism has not required personal bilingualism, in much of English-Canada it has operated to encourage it. This encouragement of personal bilingualism has in turn created the illusion for some that French is "taking over," or that bilingualism policies are a deliberate affront to the abilities and culture of unilingual English-Canadians. Language here has tended to merge with class and education differences, and with the resentments these differences themselves can cause. French-language education tends to be more widely available to the children of urban Canadians, and to those of middle-class urban Canadians who attend school board meetings, encourage early learning in their children, and keep themselves informed of school options. It tends to be less available to the children of rural Canadians, of immigrant Canadians for whom English is a second language, and of families preoccupied with daily financial struggle.

In Quebec, the effects of the policy of institutional bilingualism were strongly modified by the province's own concurrent French-affirmative legislation. Because of the widespread use of English throughout North America in government and business, by the 1960s a high proportion of professionals in Quebec were already bilingual. Particularly in Montreal, English was frequently the language of management, and often of the workplace itself. Bilingualism in Quebec, rather than being viewed, as it was in parts of English-Canada, as a means of fostering national unity and linguistic fairness, was viewed instead as a threat to the survival of French-language culture. A series of Quebec legislative bills — Bill 63 in 1969, Bill 22 in 1974, Bill 101 in 1977, and Bill 178 in 1990 — declared the province to be administratively unilingual, banned commercial signs in languages other than French, legislated French as the language of the workplace, barred the children of immigrants from publicly funded English-language schools, and in effect removed many of the causes of voluntary bilingualism among francophones. English was no longer a necessary skill for finding employment with a Quebec-based multinational company, or the provincial government. Its acquisition was no longer encouraged by advertising, or by the growth of an immigrant-fed English-speaking community.

■

So, how is her French? Better, actually, than I was expecting. Last September, I had a two-hour

> interview with Ms. Campbell, but we talked mostly in English.... Judging from the few words she had rather shyly uttered at the beginning of our meeting, I was under the impression that an interview conducted in French would drag painfully. (Lysiane Gagnon)

Like our country's 1969 policy of institutional bilingualism, the expectation that our national leaders should be able to speak both English and French is a relatively new thing. As recently as the prime ministerships of John Diefenbaker and Lester Pearson, English-Canadian political leaders were forgiven for not being able speak more than a few perfunctory, badly accented French phrases. Usually they delegated most of their campaigning in Quebec to francophone "lieutenants" like Leon Balcer, Lionel Chevrier, or Guy Favreau. On the other hand, francophone leaders of national parties, like Wilfrid Laurier, Louis St. Laurent, or Pierre Trudeau, have traditionally been 'required' to be bilingual by the necessities of winning both party support of their leadership and English-Canadian voter support of their party. Before the 1960s, a party leader needed the direct support only of English-speaking Canada to become prime minister.

The change to the present expectation that a national party leader should have at least some competence in both languages was caused in part by the same forces that brought about the Official Languages Act. Unhappiness in Quebec at having what seemed to be second-rate status in Canada, at having the use of French eroded by multinational business, at seeing immigrants overwhelmingly choose to enlarge the anglophone Quebec community, the fear of becoming a minority culture within their own province, led to the various and now all-too-familiar Quebec demands for more provincial power — demands that manifested themselves to English-Canadians as "The

Quiet Revolution," "sovereigntism," "separatism," the Parti Québécois, the "RIN," and the "FLQ." These demands in turn raised the general level of awareness of francophone culture throughout Canada, caused the Pearson government in 1963 to launch the Royal Commission on Bilingualism and Biculturalism, a commission that itself launched the "bi and bi" words into common Canadian usage. Television changed the ways in which political campaigns were conducted, allowing the leader much greater visibility and more vicariously "direct" ways of communicating with voters across Canada. New bilingual leaders that these new circumstances brought to prominence — Pierre Trudeau, Jean Chrétien, Brian Mulroney, René Levesque, Robert Bourassa, David Peterson — in turn raised public expectations of the language abilities of Canadian leaders. Trudeau and Mulroney were especially influential models, in that neither was perceived as specifically "francophone" or "anglophone" by either community. Both could speak unaccented versions of either language. When detested and vilified, both were detested and vilified for their policies rather than for their language or ethnicity.

■

> I let Calgary be Kim's night to shine. She speaks French like the Queen — very slowly. (John Long, quoted in *The Globe and Mail*, 10 May 1993)

The embarrassment many Canadians suffered during the recent Conservative leadership campaign at the fumbling attempts of eleventh-hour candidate John Long to say a few coherent words in French shows the extent to which English-Canada has been redefined and reconstructed by the tumultuous cultural and linguistic events of the 1960s. Although Long left the CBC's English-language translator guessing at what he may have meant, perhaps even fabricating a meaning, he was no less articulate in French than Diefenbaker, Pearson, or Ed Broadbent had been before him. The change in the generally assumed ground rules for party-leadership had already knocked several prominent Tories with weak French skills — Michael Wilson, Barbara McDougall, Don Mazankowski — from the contest. Ability in French was less critical for the three candidates who entered the race, for career and policy reasons, without hope of winning — Jim Edwards, Patrick Boyer, Garth Turner — although even these, to their credit, felt compelled by the new national decency to speak French as well as possible, and more often than formally required.

For Kim Campbell, however, as the one anglophone candidate in the race with a chance of winning, high competence, even some charm, in French was essential. Her only real competition in the race, Jean Charest, was not merely a good, mid-level cabinet minister, not merely the only francophone candidate, and not merely a practiced politician skilled in the kinds of 45-second sound-bites the leadership debates were founded on. He was also a splendid example of the new Canadian leadership model, prototyped by Trudeau and put into full production by Mulroney. He was a transnationally cultured man, a "transparent" francophone, who spoke English as she is spoken in Calgary, and French as she is spoken in Sherbrooke. Although he was perceived initially by the media as a token candidate, a stalking horse drafted by Mulroney to make the leadership selection appear less like a coronation and more like a battle, he was in fact the most dangerous to Campbell of any of the possible francophone contenders.

■

In B.C. novelist George Bowering's *Caprice*, the title character, a young francophone woman from St. Foy, Quebec, who has come to British Columbia to avenge the murder of her brother, has fallen in love with a local schoolteacher, Roy Smith. Smith implores her to give up her vendetta. "Caprice, you are a poet, not a gunman," he says. "You were not made for this sort of thing. You went to a sister's school overlooking the St. Lawrence River. You drank coffee in tiny cups in Paris." Here we can see another strong Canadian meaning attached to French language and culture, one that English-Canadians both share with other anglophone cultures and which they have made a special part of their own lives. This meaning exists side by side with images of "frogs," "frenchies," and "pea-soupers" with which anglophone bigots have also associated the Québécois. Here French is the language of poetry, elegance, romantic vistas, fine wine, demitasses of exquisitely brewed coffee.

This is the French that has become associated with "Kim Campbell." It is not an awkward, workaday Joe Clark or Ed Broadbent French, laboriously acquired in language labs to enable political advancement. It is not a transparent, 'natural' French, equivalent to the transparent English of Trudeau, Mulroney, and Charest. It is the French, rather, of almost-high culture, of the internationally-travelled student, self-acquired along with good taste in wine, art, and fashion. In the "Kim Campbell" mythology, it connects with reports that she dabbles in oil painting, plays a cello, enjoys opera, and once had ambitions to be a concert cellist. It connects also with the casual international student life implied by the early years of her postgraduate biography: a year at the University of Oregon, three years at the London School of Economics, three months visiting the Soviet Union, a marriage that terminates her LSE studies without a degree. Class with just the right amount of imperfection. As Lysiane Gagnon concludes about what she embarrassedly and belatedly discovers is Campbell's extensive French, "The fact that she was speaking a language she hasn't completely mastered might have made her look a little less self-assured than she usually is, and this brought an added element of charm to her performance."

This kind of French — language as a sign of unstudied sophistication — fits uneasily, however, into the Conservative party and only somewhat easily into Canada. As in the case of English-Canadian French immersion enrollment, there are strong signs of class conflict among the Tories. The contemporary Conservative party in Canada has been frequently described by political scientists as a loose coalition of regional and class interests — among these an Ontario business community popularly known as "Bay Street," Quebec nationalists affiliated in the 1984 and 1988 federal elections with the Parti Québécois, fiscal conservatives from prairie cities, and Christian "fundamentalists" from the rural prairies. Prairie members of the federal caucus were among the most vocal opponents of Campbell's gun-control legislation; far-right members of the constituency association of Health Minister Jake Epp, unhappy about the party's inactivity on abortion legislation, are said to have been partly responsible for his decision to retire from politics. Signs that this prairie segment of the party is unhappy with Campbell were evident early in the leadership campaign — in Albertan Jim Edwards' candidacy and *Alberta Report*'s characterization of Campbell as "fashionably left-wing, pro-gay, pro-feminist." Edwards supporters cheered during the Calgary leadership debate when he announced he would not be speaking French that evening, obliging him to very gently rebuke them.

Because of its evocation of the other class indicators that resonate in Kim Campbell's public history — her father having been a crown attorney, her two professional husbands, her strong support from Bay Street Tories like Michael Wilson and Perrin Beatty — Campbell's relaxed and colloquial French seems also to do her little good among both left and far-right opponents of her party. Reform Party members consider her to have little grasp of rural issues, and read with delight quotations from her 1986 interview with *The Vancouver Sun*'s Gillian Shaw, in which she declared "I genuinely like ordinary people" (in *Alberta Report*), and then infelicitously added that she didn't socialize with them because "I suppose they would find me boring, as I would them." NDP organizers are reported by *The Toronto Star*'s George Oake to "gleefully remember how she addressed her skid-row audience during the 1983 provincial election campaign."

> "I know that a lot of you have had disappointments in your life," said Campbell, who dressed down for the occasion by wearing blue jeans and a jacket. "I've been disappointed too. You see at one point in my life I desperately wanted to be a concert cellist."

■

Because of its association with 'high' culture, however, the ability to speak French remains extremely important to the Conservative party as a whole. As a cereal-box sign of Canadianness, it acts as a guarantee that we are not yet Americans, no matter how many free trade agreements with the United States the Conservatives have negotiated. For a party not known for its nationalism or its defence of culture, a prime minister who can make Canadians feel proud by being more functionally bilingual than the current American president is a major asset. Even under Brian Mulroney, Canadians could believe that although their prime minister imposed taxes on books, and was twice outfoxed at free trade bargaining tables, he was still at least more *cultured* than any one of three U.S. presidents.

To the extent that such an image of culture has become for many Tories almost a prime ministerial job requirement, only Campbell or Charest, from among the leadership candidates, could have been envisioned by the party as a whole as qualified for the position. A similar advantage is gained by the party through its leader's French competency in relation to general economic policies. As a sign of sophistication and culture, competence in French tends to subvert the party's reputation as a philistine, pragmatic, heartless, business-oriented cabal. The party may claw back the pensions of the more affluent elderly; it may limit eligibility for Unemployment Insurance; it may damage the Canada Council for the Arts by reducing its funding and attempting to merge it with the Social Sciences and Humanities Research Council; it may renege on implementing universal daycare; it may dissolve the Economic Council of Canada; it may reward its own party-hacks with patronage appointments; it may drastically underfund the Public Lending Right fees that are for many authors their major source of income; its leadership candidates may threaten to allow user-fees for medicare. Nevertheless, the Prime Minister can chat in fluent French to reporters in New York or Moscow, or to French government officials in Paris. Our government may seem to us to be a group of self-serving cheapskates, but they are at least *stylish* cheapskates.

■

> She isn't as fluently bilingual as her husband but she feels she copes quite well in English. Is she as bilingual as leadership hopeful Kim Campbell? Dionne [Jean Charest's wife Michèle Dionne] laughed. "The definition of bilingualism isn't the same across the country." (Rollande Parent)

> While people like Prime Minister Mulroney and Liberal leader Jean Chrétien always make a point of speaking both official languages no matter where they are to symbolize the bilingual nature of the country, Campbell does not.
>
> In English Canada, she often speaks only English and in Quebec only French. (Edison Stewart)

In the spring of 1993, on the other side of the French language issue in Canada — Quebec — controversy over the enforced unilingualism of commercial signs is reawakening. A commission of the United Nations has found the sign-law provisions of Bill 178 to contravene basic human rights. The provincial Liberal party has voted to relax somewhat the sign laws. The Liberal government appears ready to adopt this as policy. The anglophone candidates for the federal Tory leadership may speak French, and symbolically reassure Québécois of the equal status of their language, but what kind of Quebec French do they speak? Is it a self-protecting, nationalist French, that would allow limits on anglophone expression and education? Or would it be a tolerant French — a more confident French, some would say — that would relax the restrictions on the use of English? A mischievous question from the audience of the leadership campaign's second debate, in Montreal, asked for the candidates to comment on Quebec Liberals' new policy. John Long took the opportunity to attack official bilingualism offering, in a mixture of equally halting French and English, the extreme right-wing English-Canadian argument that bilingualism damages national unity. Jean Charest launched a high-minded federalist peroration on the duties of a prime minister to hold office for all Canadians, to defend equally the language rights of francophones in Saskatchewan, Manitoba, Ontario, and Quebec, and of anglophones in Quebec, and said he welcomed the relaxing of Quebec's language laws.

Kim Campbell replied tersely that she would not interfere in the internal politics of Quebec, that she would not repeat the arrogance of Pierre Trudeau.

Here the anglo speaks Quebec nationalist French. The "franco" speaks federalist French. Ironically, the anglo's position here, which encourages the unilingualism policies of Quebec's Bill 101, is also close to the position of John Long who, by abolishing bilingualism, would leave Quebec unilingually French and English Canada unilingually English. The franco's position is one which would make him equally unpopular in rural Quebec and in rural Ontario and Alberta. The morning after the debate, most Canadian newspapers commented on Campbell's having affiliated herself here with the Quebec linguistic nationalists who had helped Mulroney get elected, and suggested that Charest had been the debate's overall winner. In terms of its influence on delegate selection, however, it was not at all clear which candidate — how you say? — had zee hedge.

Photo: Canada Wide Feature Services Limited

CHAPTER VI:
Campbellmania

> Her campaign has all the markings of the front-runner's style — keep your face in sight while you keep your head down — more suited to the Cirque du Soleil than the Race for the Roses. ("Campbell-babble," *The Globe and Mail*)

The first public mention of a thing called "Campbell-mania" came in the days immediately before and after Campbell's March 26 launch of her leadership bid. Patrick Doyle of *The Toronto Star*, under the headline "Kim craze irks some PCs," and a photo of a grinning Campbell escorted by country-music star George Fox, wrote on March 22 that "Canada's fascination" with Campbell, its "Kim-mania," had "driven off a host of serious contenders and all but eclipsed the other candidates." Although his article purported to convey complaints about Campbell's still unofficial campaign, its effect was to confirm that a "Kim craze" was in fact under way. On the same day, *Maclean's*, reporting an enormous amount of support for Campbell, suggested that some Vancouver residents were "unmoved by the talk of Campbell-mania." On April 1 and 3 in *The Globe and Mail*, came the word "Campbell-mania" itself, first in Pauline Couture's Québécois Voices column, "Charting the course of Campbellmania," and next in Lysiane Gagnon's comment that the staging of candidate Campbell's first public appearance in Quebec appeared calculated to create "vibrant images of swelling Campbellmania."

That there was general Canadian "fascination" with Campbell underlying and provoking these reports, however, seemed doubtful. The "Campbellmania," if there was such a thing, was mainly restricted to the Conservative party. The word merely pointed to the early success of Campbell and her organizers in locking up the support of major elements of the party, particularly the fundraisers so important to a Canada-wide high-profile campaign. It was this success that was "irking" some PCs, not some tidal wave of public support for Campbell.

The term, however, was also a transparent reference to the 1968 electoral campaign of Pierre Trudeau, to "Trudeaumania." It informed Canadians that at least some Tories and some journalists saw a strong resemblance, not so much between Campbell and Trudeau, as between the Canadian responses to "Campbell" and "Trudeau." It implied that the two phenomena were, in some sense, inherently similar. Its use by Patrick Doyle and the Conservatives he was describing was ironic and deprecating; "Campbell" to them was like "Trudeau" in being a show business illusion — a "curiosity," Barbara McDougall hinted — rather than a candidate who had been legitimated (like her) by a long history of party service. But its uses by *Maclean's* and, a week later, by Couture appeared designed to flatter Campbell. "Ms Bissonette thinks that Campbellmania may reflect a desire by the electorate to change the guard more than to change policies radically.... The Campbell record, she says, shows an ability to govern at the centre...."

The quick movement of the Campbellmania concept from irony to praise is not itself without its ironies. Pierre Trudeau was, from 1968 to 1984, the Tory nemesis who three times defeated the election campaigns of Robert Stanfield, and who rose from political retirement to humiliate Joe Clark. His National Energy Policy outraged the Conservative governments of Alberta. His liberalization, while minister of justice, of laws affecting homosexuals, and his delight in beautiful women demonstrated throughout his prime ministership, incited right-wing opponents to launch vicious rumour campaigns about his sexuality. Nevertheless, the comparison to Trudeau is one that, from time to time, Campbell has herself encouraged, and that could well stay with her, at least in the short term.

■

> To those who are astonished by her rapid rise, she replies that it took only two years for Pierre Trudeau to become Minister of Justice. (Michel Vastel)

In many ways, the national meanings of "Trudeau" and "Trudeaumania" have become larger than the Liberal party or than the particular policies of the Trudeau government. Trudeau himself was an individualistic thinker, seldom bound by Liberal party history or ideology, and often able to persuade the party to follow his personal goals. His name has become a synonym for remarkable success, and personal persistence — as Campbell uses it above — a benchmark by which she and others can be measured. For many observers in the 1970s, it came to epitomize the possibility of Canadian "greatness." To Bruce Powe, Trudeau was "the most implacable visionary" the country had yet produced. His horsemanship, debating skills, diving prowess, ability on a trampoline, ready wit, easy handling of a canoe, social charm — all intact at age sixty — transcended his political programmes and became attached to the fantasy lives of many Canadians — many of whom might not vote for him, but would nevertheless welcome being more like him. So even when the ultra-conservative *Alberta Report* writes of Campbell that

> [in] that socially significant portfolio [Justice] she distinguished herself by introducing 28 bills in 35 months, and getting 26 passed — more than any justice minister since Ron Basford, the bald, pipe-smoking MP who also represented Vancouver Centre; and more than the activist Pierre Trudeau in the 1960s, to whom Ms. Campbell is often compared ...

the comparison runs in at least two directions.

In fact, lurking behind these vaguely insinuated reservations of *Alberta Report* — the "pipe-smoking" of Basford, the "activism" of Trudeau — is not only the understanding that both justice ministers were Liberals but also that Trudeau's term in particular was marked by legislation that relaxed laws affecting sexual behaviour. As in the case of Campbell's association, as justice minister, with the decriminalization of abortion, the rape-shield law, and an attempt to enact homosexual rights, Trudeau's association with legislation that liberalized the grounds for divorce and which relaxed sanctions against homosexuality and abortion lent an aura of sexual excitement to his name. Both his personal life and various instances of his public behaviour came to be perceived as connected to this sexual aura, as has tended to happen with Campbell as well. He was a bachelor, frequently seen in the company of attractive women. He owned an expensive Mercedes sports car. He boldly displayed his trim, athletic body. Single women were known to be overnight guests at 24 Sussex Drive.

■

> Her large house surrounded by oak trees, overlooking Vancouver harbour, seems to her horribly empty. And her Ottawa apartment is too small for her

to have her piano moved in. "When I think that Henry Kissinger found power to be an aphrodisiac," she once said laughingly to a woman-friend. (Michel Vastel)

It seems to me extremely unlikely, however, that "Campbellmania" could take precisely the form that "Trudeaumania" took in the 1960s and 70s. Not only are the personal differences between Campbell and Trudeau too great, but the economic and cultural circumstances of the decades in which their "mania" arose are also widely different. If we leaf back today through the photos of Trudeau in his heyday, one thing that strikes us strongly is the image of affluence they project. Photo after photo of Trudeau in black-tie, accompanied by women in evening dress. Photo after photo also of Trudeau expensively attired for sport — wet suits for surfing, a morning coat for playing billiards, fringed buckskins for riding in the West, a fur-lined Mother Hubbard for Arctic canoeing. Numerous photos of leisurely travel to exotic places. In the prosperity before the Middle East oil crisis of 1973, such signs did not seem out of place attached to a national or world leader. These were boom years, and the Trudeau image appeared merely to reflect back to Canadians their new image of themselves as an affluent, world-class society. But in the deficit and debt crisis of Canada in the 1990s, projecting such an image would be extremely difficult politically for a Canadian prime minister. A politician in the 90s is more likely to wish to present herself, like Ontario's Bob Rae, as he cuts his own salary, or Alberta's Ralph Klein as he cancels his government pension — as sharing in the general "pain" of the times rather than as cavorting above it.

As for the known differences between Trudeau and Campbell, these appear profound. Superficially there is a resemblance. They have both been considered intellectuals:

Trudeau for his classical education at Jean-de-Brébeuf and graduate study at Harvard and the London School of Economics; Campbell for her undergraduate degree in political science and for having also done graduate work at LSE. "Kim Campbell révèle une profondeur intellectuelle exceptionelle" exclaims Michel Vastel. Both trained as lawyers. Both came to mainstream politics from the outside — Trudeau from a decade as a socialist and activist opponent of Quebec's Duplessis government, Campbell as a Social Credit member of the B.C. legislature. Even within these similarities, however, are stark differences. Trudeau's strict classical education at a Jesuit college and Campbell's public schooling at Prince of Wales high. Trudeau's practising law for many years, and Campbell's becoming an elected politician while still in law school. Trudeau's early political activity being activist and oppositional; Campbell's taking place within an ideologically conservative party long in power.

Some have argued that the most important similarity between the two is that both are "outsiders." Martin Goldfarb is quoted by Rosemary Speirs as arguing that "Canada's 'closed shop' parliamentary system causes voters to look for 'outsiders'."

> "Pierre Trudeau was the loner. Brian Mulroney came from private industry. Kim Campbell's relatively new to politics, she's a woman, she's from B.C. She's so outside she's a new hero figure."

Indeed both were relatively new to their parties when they began to seek the leadership. Both represented a refreshing change — Trudeau in his style, Campbell in her combination of gender and region — from the usual range of candidates. But while Trudeau came to the Liberals and the leadership with a well-defined ideological past, and with plans to employ a policy of national bilingualism to defeat Quebec nationalism, there is little evidence in

Campbell's history or in her current proposals that she offers such precision. Her having joined the B.C. Social Credit party while also supporting liberalized abortion suggests at best a pragmatic approach to career and government. Judy Steed's inquiry into Campbell's political past discovered a fellow UBC student councillor who recalled that he "never had the feeling that she was left of centre.... She had an extremely good sense of when to take a stand on a popular issue." *Alberta Report* finds a losing candidate for a seat on the Vancouver School Board who remembers his rival as having "no strong ideological bent ... Kim does face-shifts too often for a party to follow her." Moreover, Campbell has never been a "loner" in the sense that Goldfarb describes Trudeau. She has been more often the protégée of strong men — of the husband who preceded her in her school board seat, of Bill Bennett whom she served as office director, of Brian Mulroney who is rumoured by some (see Dalton Camp, "Tory hopefuls' choice" and Anthony Wilson-Smith, "In Mulroney's Grip") to have intervened more than once to ensure the success of her most recent candidacy. In the first two leadership debates, her performance often had the unsettling effect of revealing itself to be just that — a performance, as if she were reading lines that had been scripted for her, and hoping for the approval of someone offstage when the debate was over. Only in brief flashes has she mirrored the kind of supremely self-confident, exhibitionist, risk-taking outsider that inspired Trudeaumania.

■

But is this too close, too exacting, a comparison of Campbellmania and Trudeaumania? Even as I extend this comparison I am aware of how bizarre it may be to expect the public images of a man and woman in such a gender-marked society as ours to reflect meaningfully one on the other. The very coining of the words "Kim-mania" and

"Campbellmania," with their baggage of ironic or serious comparison to Trudeau, have been in a sense sexist and demeaning to Campbell. The comparison was a game she could not win. An attractive woman politician who strutted her sexuality like Trudeau once strutted his would be judged by the same double standards that women encounter elsewhere in our culture. As a male friend once joked to me in my youth, "If I were a girl, I'd be a whore." Or as Vastel writes, "One trembles to think what would be said if, like him, Kim Campbell entertained lovers at the official residence!" In a systematically sexist political system such as ours, in which more than 80% of the elected officials, most of the party officials, and nearly all of the party money-raisers and strategists are male, in which the two largest parties are overwhelmingly funded by a male-dominated legal and business community, is it surprising that, if a woman like Campbell has approached the peak of power, she should have done it with male assistance? Judy LaMarsh's route to political office began in her father's law office and in her becoming his law partner. Flora MacDonald's began with nine years of service as secretary and executive secretary to male directors of the Conservative's national office. Sheila Copp's way into political life was prepared by the repeated electoral successes of her father, Vic Copps, as mayor of Hamilton.

Further, is it odd in a culture that esteems macho behaviour in men, but suspects it in women — a culture that eventually nicknamed Trudeau the "gunslinger" — that Trudeau should be able to develop strong oppositional stances, or learn to dominate the Liberal caucus with his individually conceived policies, while Campbell should gain a reputation as a pragmatist or opportunist, or should launch her leadership campaign by promising to initiate "a politics of inclusiveness" and to treat party members "with collegiality and respect"? However one views her politics, one should not forget that she is obliged to conduct it against a background of male norms. The "brash," "fiery," "renegade," "scrapper" Campbell that the media headlines invented after her break with Vander Zalm was a male-based conception, a conception that the sex-biased structure of Canadian politics could not give her the freedom to consistently "be." "Campbellmania" too erects a male norm that it would likely be self-destructive for her to attempt to meet.

■

> Like Pierre Trudeau, she is seen as someone who doesn't suffer fools gladly; also like Trudeau, her wit often carries the day. (Judy Steed)

> Her voice can be as aggravating as that of Pierre Trudeau when she believes, as she often does, that she has been asked a stupid question. (Michel Vastel)

> Although Kim Campbell is intelligent, well-educated and charming, she just does not seem to have what it takes to be a good prime minister.... Most people prefer a leader like former prime minister Pierre Trudeau, who stands honestly by his principles even when they happen to be unpopular. (Rory Leishman, *The London Free Press*)

Nevertheless, the comparisons between Trudeau and Campbell continue. They are made by those who like both of them, by those who mistrust both of them, and by those who prefer Trudeau. They are made by Campbell herself, during the Montreal debate, to those whom she hopes prefer her: "Kim Campbell will never allow any bureaucrat or any interest groups to revive the arrogant, domineering, centralizing federalism of the Trudeau-Chrétien years." Pierre Elliott Trudeau thus becomes a sort of defining shadow within the "Kim Campbell" persona, his strengths providing the meaning for her strengths, his limitations providing the reference points for her virtues. "Campbellmania" in a sense promises Canadians a new feminized Trudeau — vigorous, decisive, filled with sexual energy, but lacking his fabled arrogance, abrasiveness, petulance, and bull-headedness. As an image, this has a wonderful attractiveness to it. As a symbol of policy, however, it would appear to be both a travesty of Trudeau's federalism and a betrayal of Campbell's gender.

There is also a major irony here in that Pierre Trudeau should be granted enhanced political life by being made a part of the "Kim Campbell" persona. Trudeau was not only the nemesis of the Stanfield and Clark conservatives; he was also the bête noire of Brian Mulroney and the target of his hapless constitutional forays. Mulroney disturbed Canada's constitutional peace in 1989-90 in order to reopen Trudeau's 1982 Constitution Act and portray Trudeau as the prime minister who had "shut" Quebec out of the constitution. Mulroney's vision of a decentralized, deregulated Canada, open to domination by the multinational businesses that had financed his electoral campaigns, became his government's Meech Lake Accord, and was defeated by a coalition of groups that included Trudeau, Newfoundland premier Clyde Wells, and Wells' advisor (and mother of Trudeau's most recent child), the brilliant constitutional lawyer Deborah Coyne. In a sense, family man and decentralist Mulroney was thwarted by a still-swinging, septuagenarian, federalist Trudeau. In 1992 Mulroney's second attempt to achieve a "devolved" Canada, the Charlottetown Agreement, was defeated by referendum. Once again an articulate opponent of the Mulroney constitutional revisions was Deborah Coyne.

The resurgent power of the Pierre Trudeau myth, its brooding power during the recent constitutional controversies and its partial reincarnation in Kim Campbell, also suggests a sizable desire within Canadian society itself for the return of a Trudeau-like figure. Exactly why this is so is difficult to say, although it seems likely the political confusion and indirection of the Meech Lake / Charlottetown Accord years may have something to do with it. For although the economic conditions of the mid-1960s were much different from those of our own time, the political conditions were not. The Diefenbaker and Pearson governments that preceded Trudeau were consumed by their own internal quarrels and indecision, and by their own mutual dislike; Peter Newman entitled his unsettling overview of the period *The Distemper of our Times*. Today Canadians attempt to emerge from another difficult period, during which the Mulroney government became the most unpopular federal government in Canadian polling history, and both opposition leaders, Chrétien and McLaughlin, seemed powerless to gain public interest or trust. While both unemployment and the federal deficit rose, the government addressed its attention not to imaginative economic policies but to the encouragement of constitutional dissension and crisis.

Campbellmania, like Trudeaumania, may be more a symptom of malaise and a desire for change than a sign that confidence and prosperity are about to return.

■

The Jean Charest campaign's response to Campbellmania was the ironic invention of "Turtlemania." If Campbell had appeared, like Trudeau before her, to race ahead on a wave of public enthusiasm, Charest would plod along like Aesop's tortoise, and slowly but surely overtake and win. There were not too deeply hidden messages in the adoption of this image: the tortoise was steady — reliable, stable, truly conservative, unlike someone whose past of broken marriages and Social Credit membership might suggest rabbit-like flashes of enthusiasm; the tortoise was single-minded and dedicated, unlike someone else who might be flighty, unpredictable — perhaps even "hare-brained"; as well, the Charest tortoise was green, the colour of his Tory-team jacket, and the colour also of environmental friendship and of Charest's development-friendly Ministry of the Environment — emphatically not the colour of a "fiery" and sometimes "caustic" Kim Campbell.

The "Turtlemania" image, however, had the additional effect again of introducing Trudeau and "Trudeaumania" as a campaign model. Charest was also seeking a "mania," a swell of excitement about his candidacy which did indeed materialize and, in public opinion polls taken in the convention week, exceed the excitement raised by the more flamboyant Kim. Moreover, in one respect Charest indeed did resemble Trudeau — in his announced committment to a federalist Canada, and to be, as he had declared in the Montreal debate, a prime minister "for all Canadians." It was this resemblance that *L'actualité* had noted early in the campaign, and had wryly suggested made him the kind of Quebecker English-Canadians love.

> Jean Charest est un Québécois comme les Canadiens les aiment. Biculturel, c'est un jeune Pierre Trudeau, l'arrogance en moins. ("Le style Charest")

But nationalist Québécois, the article noted later, had already accused him, during the Meech Lake negotiations, of "treason."

One last thought about politicomania. In his fanciful description of pre-Christian bronze-age cultures of Britain and Wales, *The White Goddess*, poet Robert Graves portrays a culture in which, for mythic, military, and symbolic reasons, a tribe had to have a physically and sexually vigourous king. A king was ritually sacrificed at each autumn equinox, or at longer intervals as the society matured, Graves suggests, in order that a younger, stronger, and more virile king could replace him. In North American democratic societies today Graves might well find this mythic desire for a virile, athletic, sexually resonant leader displayed in such phenomena as the election of generals like Eisenhower, the rumoured liaisons of Kennedy, the public jogging exhibitions of Bush and Clinton, the fatherly interest in children of St. Laurent. In particularly dispirited times perhaps this hunger requires the carnivalesque kingship of a Pierre Trudeau. Perhaps today Canadians are indeed ready to invent a "Campbellmania."

Photo: Canapress

CHAPTER VII

Minister for the Defence

> I have the helicopters ... (Kim Campbell, at the Halifax leadership debate)

I remember as I begin this chapter that thirty years ago I worked for the Department of National Defence. I was a lecturer, later assistant professor, in English at Royal Roads Military College in Victoria, teaching courses in Utopian Literature to officer cadets for the three, then un-unified, services. If I were there now, "Kim Campbell" would be the name of my minister, and I very likely would not have thought of writing this book. What I recall most about my six years at Roads, was the widespread conviction that we were indeed training the officers for a peacekeeping Armed Forces. These were the Lester Pearson forces — his image as a Nobel Prize winner prevailed here against the neighbouring image of a United States Armed Forces, fully belligerent in Vietnam. Although the administering officer corps at Roads was uneasily divided between the older veterans of World War II and the Korean War and the younger unbloodied graduates of the college system, all seemed viscerally to understand a profound difference between the kind of soldiers we were training and the kind we were occasionally obliged to visit south of the border. One of the teaching plans that was being considered in 1969 when I left was a series of "area studies" programmes which would train officers in the languages, cultures, and histories of areas where they seemed most likely to have to serve as peacekeepers. On the other hand, whenever the tall, de Gaulle-like figure of Defence Minister Paul Hellyer had visited the college, there appeared to be little talk about curriculum, unless that curriculum implied expanded physical facilities — expanded and more splendid buildings, and more and more exotic research installations. Two of the major events at the college had been the acquisition for permanent display of a vintage tank and a Sabre jet.

When I read today about Canadian soldiers in Cyprus, Bosnia, or Somalia, I often recall my students of those days, the "utopian literature" they studied, and the utopian curricula plans the three Canadian military colleges seemed to be seeking. I wonder too why so little news of their models for military training ever reached the public. And to what extent had they been communicated to the ordinary soldiers, or to cabinet ministers.

■

Kim Campbell was moved by Prime Minister Brian Mulroney from the ministry of justice to the ministry of defence in his January 4, 1993, cabinet shuffle. The move was greeted in the media by widespread speculation about whether this was a promotion or a demotion, whether he was "clipping her wings" or aiding them. Earlier speculation about whether or not Mulroney was considering a spring retirement, and whether Campbell would be a leading contender to succeed him, was revived. Questions were raised about whether the shuffle signalled his approval or disapproval of a Campbell candidacy. The cumulative effect of the speculation, however, tended to answer its own questions. Campbell's assignment to the defence ministry did not clip her wings, but made her, as *Maclean's* titled its cover story about

Campbell two weeks later, "a rising star." Her position as "Canada's first female defence minister" had become the major story of the cabinet shuffle.

As simply a cabinet position, the defence ministry appeared to offer Campbell an ambiguous opportunity. It was a radically different sort of portfolio from the justice ministry in which Campbell had developed a reputation within the Tory party for being a reliable administrator. Justice associated its minister with social causes and issues, with both the plights of individuals like Donald Marshall and David Milgaard, and general questions of abortion, capital punishment, homosexuality, juvenile crime, and the funding of legal challenges under the Charter of Rights. It gave its minister an opportunity to attempt to present herself as sympathetic but firm, as socially responsible both in seeking increased fairness and in maintaining the protections of the law. It associated her with the daily hopes and fears of individual Canadians. In terms of the gender stereotypes of our culture, it mixed qualities traditionally associated with both feminity and masculinity: a caring about individual and systemic injustices, and a stern upholding of "law and order" standards. The defence ministry was in contrast, at least in its imagery, a traditionally masculine enterprise. It was associated with tanks, frigates, helicopters, and submarines; its budgets had a history of being viewed by journalists and socialists as thieving from social-welfare programmes. It was to this masculine image, and its ironic contrast to her own gender, that Campbell referred when she quipped to the *Maclean's* interviewers, "Don't mess with me, I've got tanks."

Moreover, the Canadian defence ministry had over the decades been a dead-end post for cabinet members. No post-war prime minister had held the portfolio. Many defence ministers, like Brooke Claxton, Ralph Campney,

Douglas Harkness, and Marcel Masse, had found the ministry to be a first step toward political oblivion. The towering and solemn Paul Hellyer, after an unsuccessful bid for the Liberal leadership in 1968, had become something of a comic figure, first attempting to found his own political party, and then running unsuccessfully as a federal Conservative candidate. Others, like Pierre Sévigny, associate defence minister in the Diefenbaker government, and Robert Coates, the first defence minister of Mulroney's government, had involved the ministry in macho scandal. Sévigny was found in 1966 to have potentially compromised the ministry by having had an affair, in 1958-61, with an attractive German immigrant, Gerda Munsinger, who was also sexually involved with a Soviet military attaché. In 1985, Coates was forced to resign the portfolio when reports circulated that he had visited a strip club in Lahr, Germany, site of Canada's NATO base, and allowed one of the women to sit on his lap. Adding to Coates' negative image were reports that his travel expenses while Minister of Defence had been excessively high.

For Campbell, however, attempting to make her way in the very masculine world of federal politics, the ministry appeared at the very least to give more balance to her image — to counter the one that circulated, negatively, in the rural fringes of the party as "pro-gay" and "pro-feminist" with a more no-nonsense one of pragmatic realities. Announced as fit to lead a ministry that directed admirals and generals, she was also being announced as fit to lead a party of corporation lawyers, financiers, lobbyists, and bagmen. Campbell herself was quick to link the move to her academic background at the London School of Economics in Soviet studies, and with her long-standing interest in international affairs. But, in an interesting move uncharacteristic of Canadian defence ministers, despite Canada's long history in international peacekeeping, she was also quick to maintain a link between her new ministry and her previous association with social policy. The defence forces she was taking charge of were, to her, peacekeeping troops, who could be sent out to bring an activist justice to a rapidly destabilizing international world. Pointing to the results of the collapse of the Soviet empire, she told the *Maclean's* interviewers "For the first time in my lifetime we have the capacity to make some real changes." The interviewers themselves thought they could detect a Mulroney re-election strategy at work here. "*Maclean's* has learned," they declared,

> that Mulroney plans to build a key election platform around the combined forces of Campbell and External Affairs Minister Barbara McDougall. Aided by General de Chastelain, appointed last week as Canada's ambassador to the United States, the two cabinet ministers are to merge Canada's separate defence and foreign policies into a comprehensive international policy that likely will include a reassessment of the country's traditional peacekeeping role.

■

Prior to Campbell's appointment, defence was not a high-profile portfolio. Few Canadians would be able to recall the name of the defence minister whom Campbell replaced. There had been some controversy over the EH-101 helicopter purchase, but that had been framed in the media and in Opposition questioning as a government programme, rather than one of a particularly obtuse or far-sighted defence minister. The sending of peacekeeping troops to Croatia, Bosnia, and Somalia had been relatively popular foreign policy initiatives not closely tied to national defence. General Lewis MacKenzie's service as UN field commander in Bosnia, his criticism of the weak communications links between his troops and their UN supervisors in New York, and his surprise retirement had only briefly involved the ministry in media questioning. Once Campbell declared her leadership candidacy these public conceptions of the EH-101 programme and the peacekeeping ventures changed utterly. This change was largely the work of the Liberal and NDP Opposition, who began focussing their questions about these issues almost exclusively on Campbell. In part, this strategy appeared aimed at associating her with the risks, failures, and limitations of these policies. It also seemed designed to portray her as a negligent minister. Obliged by the requirements of the leadership campaign to be absent from the Commons most days of the week, she could not be there to answer the questions that the Opposition now chose to address to her.

The message created by the strategy, however, was one that the Opposition is unlikely to have wished. It presented Campbell as the leadership candidate the opposition parties most feared, and confirmed reports like that of Allan Fotheringham that her candidacy had put the Liberals into a "stunned funk." It increased the number of times her name and face appeared in the national media, and particularly disadvantaged Charest, about whose environment ministry the Opposition asked virtually no questions, and about whose equally lengthy absences from the Commons they expressed no indignation. Charest, the Opposition's inattention implicitly told the country and Tory delegates, was a nonentity not worthy of attack; Campbell, on the other hand, had already succeeded Mulroney as the target of their wrath.

■

> Mr. Mulroney made clear Canada's opposition to the move being considered by Washington.

> "How could you be bombing the Bosnian Serbs while leaving British peacekeepers on the ground in Bosnia...?"
>
> Mr. Mulroney also had a sharp rebuke for a senior U.S. senator who said Europe's go-slow policy on Bosnia amounted to "moral rape" and hypocrisy. (*The Globe and Mail*, 12 May 1992)

Not unpredictably, the Conservative caucus responded to the Opposition attack by protecting its leading candidate. Supply and Services Minister Paul Dick, House Leader Harvie André, and even External Affairs Minister McDougall rose to answer the Opposition questions. One of the most interesting responses, however, was that of the Prime Minister, who transformed what had appeared to be a farewell, glad-handing tour of European capitals in early May into a campaign against American-proposed bombing of Bosnian Serb gun and supply lines. The anti-American tone of his speeches astonished journalists, who had become accustomed to a Mulroney who enjoyed the company of Americans and prized his friendships with Presidents Reagan and Bush. The surprise vehemence of Mulroney's statements, and the surprise substance in a foreign tour which political columnists and cartoonists had previously dismissed as a personal indulgence, and an abuse of taxpayers' dollars, quickly overshadowed the questions raised by opposition critics about the safety of Canadian troops in Bosnia, and about the killing of civilians by Canadian peacekeepers in Somalia.

There has been considerable media interest in the Prime Minister's role in the leadership campaign. Was Kim Campbell Mulroney's personal choice as his successor? Was the campaign, as *Maclean's* suggested on March 29, "in Mulroney's grip"? Was he controlling the campaign by controlling the party's money-raisers, directing them at first to channel most of their money to Campbell and later, when it appeared she would run away with the nomination, directing that some — but not "enough" — money be diverted to Charest, so that the appearance and drama of a close contest could be created? To these questions one might also add this one: Did Mulroney transform his European holiday into a headline-grabbing anti-American crusade in order to divert attention from the Opposition's attacks on Campbell, and to substitute himself and his impeccable high-profile European connections for her necessarily perfunctory replies? Was this one of his rewards to Campbell for her having refused in the leadership debates to break with caucus discipline by criticizing its 1993 budget, its helicopter purchase, or its Quebec language policies?

Mulroney's statements not only pre-empted much of the coverage the Somalia killings had been receiving in the media but also changed the sorts of questions that were being asked about the Canadians in Srebrenica. No longer was it a question of whether the Defence Minister was watching over the safety of those Canadian troops; rather it was a question of how successful a powerful Canadian-European alliance, welded together by chiefs of state, could be in thwarting an adventurist American "peace" initiative.

■

> Canada may not be able to send more ground troops to the former Yugoslavia, Defence Minister Kim Campbell said today. (*The London Free Press*, 6 May 1993)

This statement was not made in the context of a campaign appearance but to a meeting of the Commons Defence Committee. It was reported, however, under large headlines, in numerous Canadian papers. "The important thing is to recognize that we don't have a blank cheque, we don't have an unlimited capacity to participate," Campbell was reported to have continued. A major contribution that the defence portfolio gave to Kim Campbell was an additional vocabulary with which to discuss economic issues which had become the heart of the leadership campaign. At each debate and city stop of the campaign, questions about the deficit, the national debt, and how the need to reduce these might affect social programmes were posed to the candidates. There was virtual unanimity among them that the deficit must be reduced and eventually eliminated, and the debt thus kept from rising. Campbell's new portfolio allowed her to extend the grounds of this economic argument into a historic area of national achievement and pride. Canadians have repeatedly been made to think of their nation as a peacekeeping nation, despite the recurrent tension between this image and that of the major heavy weapons systems — tanks, frigates, Sabre jets — the military also recurrently takes pride in acquiring. Canadians, like the 1960s officer-cadets at Royal Roads, are told of how this history began in the Suez crisis of 1956, and in Lester Pearson's Nobel Prize-winning diplomacy. They are told that Canada has participated in every United Nations peacekeeping force since that year. Even during Prime Minister Mulroney's recent tour, Canadians are complimented by Russian President Boris Yeltsin for their peace-keeping "expertise." Campbell's message was that this historic national symbol is, like universal medicare, pensions, and Unemployment Insurance, also jeopardized by the deficit crisis. We not only stand to lose social programmes, as all the candidates have been saying, but we also risk ceasing to be the "peacekeeping" Canadians we have become accustomed to being. As well, Campbell was enabled by her new portfolio to broaden the theatre of her campaign. She could exemplify her leadership-quality insights in other contexts than mere constituency luncheons and televised debates. She could earn national headlines for reasons other than her candidacy.

Campbell's association with the killings of Somalis by soldiers of the Canadian Airborne Regiment had a similar ironically positive effect, even though the bare facts of the cases had far more damaging potential for her. Four Somalis were killed by members of the Airborne Regiment on peacekeeping duty in northern Somalia. Two of these were deemed by regimental officers to have been killed according to the Armed Force's "rules of engagement." A third was found beaten to death in his cell, after having been detained for unauthorized entry into the military compound. A fourth was reported by the chief medical officer of the regiment — in a letter to his wife — to have been shot in the back and subsequently at closer range in the neck or head. Under a liberally constructed doctrine of ministerial responsibility, Campbell could be viewed as remotely responsible for these deaths, although no one appears to have made such an argument. However, since she was not the defence minister who posted the regiment to Somalia, she could not really be held morally responsible for having sent a trigger-happy group of soldiers to do a task for which they were unsuited. Accumulating evidence, in fact, began to suggest that the Airborne were a unit more trained in hairtrigger violence than in the diplomatic dissuasion of looters. Later evidence suggested that the unit attracted tough and aggressive soldiers who took pride in their stamina and self-perceived savagery, and that some of these were also members, or had been members, of racist white-power organizations. But as the current minister of record she could be held responsible for how these deaths were investigated — for one of them appearing to have been covered up until the medical officer wrote about it to his wife, and for continuing to allow a suspected Nazi sympathizer to serve in the regiment.

To an extent, the recentness of Campbell's appointment as defence minister, and the probability of her soon not being defence minister, both operated to confuse the public presentation of the Somalia issue. The previous defence minister was the one responsible for this regiment being in Somalia, and for the aggressive standards under which it had been trained in Canada, but the Opposition was not interested in attacking him. It was very interested in attacking and discrediting Campbell, but had few persuasive arguments to bring against her. She had failed, the Opposition claimed, to ensure that Parliament and the public were properly informed of each of the incidents. But it was not clear to a public unsophisticated in parliamentary principle how she could be held guilty of not having informed Parliament of something of which she had not been fully informed herself — any more than she could be held guilty of having personally killed the two Somalis. Moreover, there were reports that she had attempted to resign as defence minister when she launched her campaign — that she had not wished to be both defence minister and leadership candidate — and that she had only been prevented from resigning by Mulroney's insistence that both she and Charest be bound by cabinet membership to existing policy. Her very absences from the house suggested that she was less than the full-time defence minister the Opposition seemed to believe it was attacking.

Campbell's own responses to the attacks further confused the overall presentation by being procedural, legalistic, and moral. She could not comment on the specifics of the killings because a defence minister is a kind of high court judge in the Canadian military justice system, and can expect to be called to rule on such cases in the event of appeal. She could not appoint an investigatory board to look into the killings because such a board might prejudice military justice proceedings already in process. She told Parliament on April 26 that she was appointing a general board of inquiry into the deployment, discipline, and "professional values and attitudes" of the Airborne Regiment. She was "instituting a review of our recruiting policy." She deplored the deaths of the Somalis. She declared racism in the armed forces to be "not acceptable." The success of this strategy lay, ironically, both in her not being regularly in Parliament and in her not responding directly or politically to her attackers. The responses had overtones of being primeministerial. She too, they implied, shared the high moral ground her critics presented themselves as speaking from. She too was shocked by racism. But the perfunctory and legalistic rhetoric of the announcement suggested the conscientiousness and morality of a railroad timetabler.

Moreover, by the mere association of the killings and a possible cover-up with the "Kim Campbell" name, damage was done. "Homicides en Somalie: l'opposition veut la démission de Kim Campbell," read a headline in *La Presse* on April 23. "Campbell faces fire: the minister put on defense on handling of Somali killings," proclaimed the *Calgary Herald* on the 24. "Campbell's department suffers another blow," read a May 8 headline in *The Toronto Star*. On May 14, the *Star* ran a cartoon of a giant "KKK" graffito at a Canadian Armed Forces base: "I thought it meant 'Kim, Kim, Kim,'" the leadership-preoccupied minister is depicted as saying. "Kim Campbell," self-styled feminist and abortion reformer, was now also, in a faint way, minister of Somali murder, minister of Armed Forces cover-up, and minister of neo-Nazi commandos.

■

The photo at the beginning of this chapter accompanied one of the articles on Campbell which appeared in the special "Campbell" issue of *Maclean's* four days before her official declaration of her leadership candidacy. The estimated $5.8 billion EH-101 helicopter purchase was another Campbell inheritance from her predecessor at defence, but one for which, as a cabinet minister at the time of the purchase decision, she shared direct responsibility. The large total price tag of the helicopter continues to make it an especially inviting target for government critics at a time of deficit crisis. There were suggestions from Campbell herself that social programmes may have to be curtailed in order for the fiscal integrity of the country to be preserved. If something needed to be sacrificed, why not helicopters before social programmes? Or helicopters before cultural programmes? Or helicopters before additional peacekeeping? "That helicopter deal could be her Achilles heel," the same issue of *Maclean's* reported a rival Liberal leader from her Vancouver Centre riding to have said.

Like Campbell's association with Somalia, the EH-101 issue is a confused one, both as a set of facts and as a symbol. To Canadians whose imaginations run toward hardware symbols, the EH-101 recalls a large number of ambiguous but confusingly powerful Canadian military objects — the corvettes built during the Second World War, the CF-100, the Canadian-designed and built destroyer-escorts of the 1950s and 60s. It recalls the debacle of the Avro Arrow; the shame of being coerced into buying the Bomarc missile, the Starfighter and the Voodoo aircraft; the navy's pride, nevertheless, in its two budget-consuming British-built aircraft carriers, the *Magnificent* and the *Bonaventure*; the continuing saga of Perrin Beatty's submarines that have been a theoretically approved purchase of the navy for almost a decade. These strong hardware symbols (witness the number of books and articles about the Arrow) periodically compete in Canadian culture — like the tank and Sabre jet competed at Royal Roads — with the similarly pride-founded images of the military as the world's best peacekeeper.

As a set of economic problems, the EH-101 is even more complex than the fabulous Arrow. Its cost is to be spread over thirteen years; cancellation would thus relieve only a small portion of the government's annual deficit problem rather than subtracting one dramatic $5.8 billion chunk. The helicopter's probable operating life is at least thirty years, which offers a defender of the purchase an even lower calculation of amortized annual cost and potential "saving." The helicopter was designed for the Cold War period as a sophisticated submarine destroyer. It is designed for a job critics say Canada is now unlikely ever to be called on to perform alone. It is also, however, its Armed Forces defenders claim, the only new helicopter of its general type in development, and the only one specifically suited to the design parameters of the frigates on which it is to be based. It is in gross dollar terms much more expensive than would be the refitting of Canada's existing helicopters, but might last twenty years longer than those helicopters, and thus in the long term cost less. Boeing, builders of the existing helicopters, dispute this, arguing that its rebuilt 'copters would last just as long. Other critics ask if Canada, in the post-Cold War period, even needs military helicopters and frigates. Defenders point to the need to protect the east coast fishery, and the navy itself promptly sends destroyers, Aurora patrol planes, and its three ancient submarines in relatively successful comic-opera operations to apprehend U.S. scallop boats poaching in Canadian waters. What price, the unstated question reads, can be placed on sovereignty? Yes, the helicopter is costly, but $2.4 billion of the expenditure will return to the struggling Canadian economy in the form of contracts with companies in at least four provinces. In addition, penalty clauses in the contracts already signed with the prime Canadian contractor, Paramax, and with the Italian-British builders, may make it more costly to cancel the contract than to honour it.

There appear to be no unequivocal answers here, no path more fiscally responsible than others, no compellingly logical course of action — or so the Mulroney government would have had us think. The journey to the present situation began more than a decade ago with the Trudeau government's decision to proceed with the frigate programme; it gathered weight and speed as the frigates were built, as committees were struck to study the accompanying helicopters. The size and ponderousness of the project made it seemingly unresponsive to changes in international politics or military probabilities. Yet for eight years the Conservative party had opportunities to change or influence it. For eight years also this government preached to Canadians about the need to reduce the annual budget deficit. While continuing tacitly to approve the helicopter purchase, it introduced clawbacks on the old age pension, and steadily cut back the provincial transfer payments that substantially fund medicare, welfare, and postsecondary education. Then — cynically or deviously, many would say — it signed contracts that now appear to foreclose all options except continuing toward the EH-101's acquisition.

■

> If she wins the leadership, she will be close to unbeatable, says Victor Huczek, president of [Campbell's] riding's federal Liberal association. "... [S]he would need an albatross around her neck to lose." That albatross, Huczek adds, may already exist: the controversial $4.4 billion defence department deal to purchase

> 50 new EH-101 helicopters. (*Maclean's*, 22 March 1993)

In the sense that it is a persistent issue in Conservative political history, the EH-101 indeed hangs around Kim Campbell's neck, the potential albatross that Huczek predicts may be found there. Moreover, she has presented herself as willing to keep it there, bragging to the delegates who attended the Halifax leadership debate that to protect Canadian waters from foreign overfishing "I have the helicopters." The delegates cheered, apparently untroubled by the image of missile-equipped helicopters, capable of detecting and destroying submerged high-speed submarines several miles away in stormy seas, being sent to confront and document the presence of fishing boats armed at best with shotguns and hunting rifles.

Curiously, no one at the Halifax debate — delegate or candidate — raised the more pressing issue of the Atlantic fisheries: fish-stock depletion and environmental damage. The $3 billion over three years that Jean Charest's environmental ministry had apparently been unable to find ways of spending was in annual terms a much larger sum than the $5.8 billion over thirty years of the helicopters. His inactivity over the defence of the environment — most visibly on the Prince Edward Island "fixed link" which could upset fish migration routes and damage shellfish beds, and on the Oldman River dam project in Alberta — and his reluctance to get involved in the Great Whale discussions had been potentially at least as damaging to Canada as anything that had transpired in Campbell's defence portfolio. Only highly visible as a minister for a few weeks around the Rio Environmental Summit, he had allowed the Ministry of the Environment to fall from public view during his years as minister, allowed its $3 billion "Green Plan" to become another broken promise, and had failed utterly to make environmental concerns a routine element in all government decisions.

Whether or not either the environment or the EH-101 will indeed function as an "albatross" for Campbell and her government, however, is a public matter, since it is only the public that can ultimately hold her responsible. But the albatross itself is a rather more troubling image than either Huczek or *Maclean's* seem to have noticed. It suggests black consequences for Canada, particularly if reports of the unbreakability of the helicopter contracts are to be believed, as much as for Campbell. In Coleridge's *The Rime of the Ancient Mariner,* from which the albatross image comes, the mariner, like Campbell, merely entangled himself with its symbolism by shooting and seizing it. It was the events that followed — the death of his shipmates, the rotting of his ship — that gave the symbol its baleful meaning. And in the end, the mariner's eternal punishment returned neither sailors nor ship to life.

Photo: Canapress

CHAPTER VIII
Electoral User Fees

> ... [W]e will unite as a family to go forward and defeat not just the enemies of the Progressive Conservative party but the enemies of Canadians — and I use that term mildly, I suppose. But those people who've been telling people that debts and deficits are not a problem, those who talk about abolishing the GST ..., those are the people we have to take on in the next federal election. (Kim Campbell)

> According to polls by the survey firm, Environics, 39 per cent of Canadians believe that their national government actually "harms the public interest." (Richard Gwyn, *The Toronto Star*)

The political identity surrounding the name of a public figure is not only made up of those images and words that family, place, chance, and the actions of others have caused to be associated with it. It is also made up of the words and images with which the public figure has personally associated his or her name. And those words and images bring with them clusters of associations that are an ongoing and routine part of the culture one lives in.

Social services in Canada have been a big part of both political debate and the self-fashioned Canadian image, at the very least since the Saskatchewan government's introduction of medicare in 1962. They have come to be understood by most Canadians as not just a "social safety net," which breaks the fall of citizens when they lose jobs or fall ill. They are seen also as socially friendly services which increase the general quality of life for the society as a whole, and which help equalize opportunities for those citizens who find themselves in circumstances, like being disabled or being a single parent, that would otherwise curtail their full participation in society. Such services now include parental benefits like the present child-care Income Tax deduction, Unemployment Insurance, Worker's Compensation, old age pensions, welfare payments, and medicare, and prospective "utopian" services like universal day-care or a guaranteed annual income. The enjoyment of such services as universal medicare, Unemployment Insurance, and the Old Age Security pension plan has accustomed most Canadians to their benefits. At the same time, however, the rising deficit, and the threat or actuality of increased taxation has made many Canadians, most particularly those in the Conservative party, ask whether these are services the country as a whole can "afford." Twenty-two and one-half billion dollars, or one-half the total expenditure, complained Tory leadership candidate Garth Turner, goes to upper-income earning Canadians.

But there is a meaning to these social services other than simply their value to their recipients or their cost to the taxpayer's purse. The services have also become valuable to Canadians as national symbols. In particular, they have become symbols that appear — like our history of peacekeeping — to differentiate Canada from the United States. Canada, we have been told many times, is a more caring country. It is a more social, cooperative, and less individualistic society than its southern neighbour. Its historic symbols have been those of social order and cohesion — the Mounted Police, the Canadian Pacific

Railway — rather than of individualist gunfighters, entrepreneurs, and charismatic leaders. That the reality has been not quite what these images suggest — that numerous entrepreneurs benefitted from the building of the CPR while "cooperative" Chinese labourers drew half-wages; that the Mounted Police often protected the rights of the propertied, from fur-traders to factory owners, while discouraging the protests of native peoples and workers who were being deprived of land or jobs — has been largely suppressed in the formation of this self-image. However, as a general truth, the proposition that Canada is a more caring society has seemed to be true. More gun-related murders occur each year in a U.S. city like Detroit or Washington than in all of Canada. Young U.S. families are obliged to borrow thousands of dollars to pay for routine childbirth expenses that in Canada are entirely paid by medicare.

The importance of this self-construction has been seen in Canadian political debate. Even as Mulroney's government was dismantling social services, it would pronounce itself to be in favour of them. In both the 1984 and 1988 election campaigns Mulroney campaigned as a defender of social benefits. In 1984, he promised that they would be fully indexed to the inflation rate, but by the next year he had de-indexed the Family Allowance and was proposing to de-index old age pensions. In 1988, he proposed expanding these benefits to include a national day-care programme, but within months of being re-elected his government was introducing legislation to "claw back" some pension and child care benefits, and to reduce Unemployment Insurance benefits. The day-care proposal slowly vanished, being deemed too expensive. Nevertheless, social programmes were still, in Mulroney's words, "a sacred trust."

In that now notorious phrase of Mulroney's can be seen

the enormous power the notion of social benefits has come to have in Canada. The phrase combines the language of law and the language of religion. A trust is one of the highest formalized duties of a lawyer, the powerful profession from whose ranks most Canadian cabinet ministers seem to come, and on which all Canadians, at some time in their lives, are obliged to rely. For breach of trust a lawyer faces almost certain disbarment — banishment and disgrace within his profession — and in many cases criminal conviction and imprisonment. A "sacred" trust elevates the concept to the level of reverence, superstition, taboo, and the threat of divine punishment. To break such a trust is to defile the altar, commit sacrilege, to invite fire, plague, and famine down upon oneself.

■

> "Ninety per cent of Canadians say they love the health-care system," [Health Minister Benoit Bouchard] said. "There is nobody who can come up with a (user fee) policy when 90 per cent of Canadians are against it." (*The Globe and Mail*, 13 May 1993)

It is one of the anomalies of Canadian politics, however, that the party governing for the past eight years, that has given Canada the phrase "sacred trust," values a different set of mythologies from those which appear to be held by most Canadians. This is a party that treasures entrepreneurship, deregulation, "family values," the "level playing field" of free trade; that believes, with Patrick Boyer, that "the best social policy is a job," and with Jean Charest that "parents are the best people to decide on care options for their children." (Both were responding to "The candidates speak on the issues" questionnaire put to them by the SouthamStar Network.) It is a party whose leader has preferred friendships with lawyers and businessmen (frequently American businessmen) and with right-of-centre U.S. presidents. The general vision of the Conservative party is founded on a concept of the capable, self-reliant, healthy, industrious individual, who encounters no economic, health, or educational barriers, and who always possesses the money necessary to buy insurance, pension, or child-care services.

A Tory candidate like Campbell, however, faces the task of selling her name and programme to a number of different constituencies: regions, ethnic groups, professionals, the unemployed, the disabled, the media, as well as to members of her own party. The recent leadership campaign has shown the contradictions to which the need to appeal to diverse or conflicting groups can lead. Jean Charest was reported to have excluded most of the French-speaking, Quebec-based media from accompanying him on campaign visits to eastern Ontario, to prevent them both from reminding the Ontarians of his French roots and from reporting to Quebecers the conciliatory, federalist messages he was delivering. To demonstrate to party delegates that she had "winnability," Campbell was obliged to appeal to a general Canadian constituency, a constituency convinced of the "sacred trust" of social programmes. At the same time, she was obliged to appeal to the individualist and fiscally conservative values of the delegates themselves in order to demonstrate that she was ideologically acceptable, as well as "winnable." Complicating the matter for her was the presence in the leadership race of candidates like Garth Turner and Jim Edwards who, with no chance of winning, could ignore the values of the general electorate and demand right-wing policies that made Campbell's own apparently more moderate proposals seem un-Conservative. Complicating it further were the voices of her Prime Minister, Brian Mulroney, and of Health

Minister Benoit Bouchard, both of whom understood from past experience the party's strategic need to appeal to the entire electorate, and who urged the candidates to stop speaking altogether about user fees for medicare.

■

> Clayoquot Sound is not just a geographic battleground for tree-spikers and blockaders to congregate in the summer. It has become a battleground of the mind, a test of whether real-life tradeoffs can be made over something as nearly spiritual as a rain forest. (Robert Sheppard)

It could be said that every politician and every political programme comes with a user fee. There are financial implications for some, if not all, of us in each decision made and each project undertaken by a government. At every election, voters check their pocketbooks, weighing how the particular array of policies offered (although not, we find, necessarily promised, not to speak of delivered) will benefit them, their children, their neighbourhoods, their sense of national pride, or in some way satisfy their own personal sense of rightness and justice. It will cost British Columbians in heritage, long-term tourism revenues, the goodwill of native peoples, to cut any of the Clayoquot trees. It will cost them in wages, tax revenues, and in the short-term economic health of west coast Vancouver Island communities not to cut the trees.

The arguments in regard to Canadian social programmes, and medicare in particular, are not so much about user fees as about how the use of these programmes is to be controlled, and in what proportions and ways users are to pay. The "user fee" concept, as it as been used by Conservative candidates, appeals to those who measure payment in dollars (or trees in dollars), and who see dollars as a sign both of an individual's worth and as a means of controlling his or her behaviour. A person who pays with his or her own money for service, in this view, will value that service. A person who must pay for service will use it judiciously, creating through this judiciousness an effective "cap" on the overall use of the service.

The difficulties with this view are numerous. For one, many people in Canada today do not have such a thing as their "own" dollars. The fee that may be charged is ultimately paid by another social programme: by welfare, mother's allowance, Unemployment Insurance. For another, "dollars" are not the only measure by which people pay to use or not use programmes. There are also illness, apathy, malnutrition, depression, family breakdown, self-hatred. For yet another, a fixed, dollar-based user fee such as the $5.00 one frequently mentioned in these discussions (as by Bouchard above), can be a variable barrier to the users themselves: a large amount to those who earn little, a modest amount to those who earn more, and a trivial amount to those who earn much. Noting this, Bouchard argued that user fees would create "two-tier systems — one for the privileged and one for the less fortunate." More likely, they would create a variably "tiered" experience of health care, intolerable for the very poor, difficult for the poor, awkward for those of modest income, manageable for the more prosperous, and easy for the rich.

■

Asked whether she would consider user fees for medicare — a challenge to the whole system of universality in Canadian social services — Campbell said she would.

"If it was the consensus of working with the provinces on how to re-jig our social programs, then yes." (Susan Delacourt, *The Globe and Mail*)

The reporter's careful handling of the wording of these sentences, and Campbell's own careful qualifying of her statement are symptomatic of the position of the Conservative party in Canada. A party historically reluctant to endorse universal social programmes, often unsympathetic to the poor (whom many rank-and-file Tories seem to feel would not be poor if, in the usual clichés, they would just work harder, look for a job, show more foresight), and unconvinced by theories of structural unemployment, cannot get itself elected by the general populace unless it presents itself, at least in words, as endorsing social programmes. Campbell thus presented herself here, at the third leadership debate in Calgary, in a kind of code. She agreed that she "would consider" user fees, thus simultaneously assuring the delegates that she would be open to such things as a restricted medicare, at the same time as she was reassuring a general audience that this isn't her idea or even her intention: it is only something she would "consider." Moreover, a user fee policy would also have to be subject to "consensus" of the provinces. "Consensus" is another code word connected to the politics of "inclusion" that Campbell had previously announced. Together, the words sound warm and congenial. But, when one thinks back to the tumultuous and frustrating months of provincial discussions that led to Meech Lake and the Charlottetown Accord, is a consensus of the provinces really likely?

Here is the political user fee the Tory delegates were asked to pay for the "winnability" of Kim Campbell. She will say the magic word "user fees," and thereby upset electorally-minded Mulroney and Bouchard, but will not definitely commit herself to them. But for the general voter there is another sort of user fee implied: voting for "Campbell" could very well lead to a surcharge on medicare.

Hidden behind these words, however, is an issue neither the Conservative party nor the electorate wish to talk about: the possible need to redraw the way wealth is distributed in Canada — a need brought into being partly by the Tories' own abrupt introduction of deregulation and free trade policies. The basic economic problem facing each level of government in Canada today is how to divide the gross national product in such a way that all services that the country believes are economically or culturally necessary — including the prevention of poverty — are paid for without the creation of new public debt. Mulroney's government, in particular, has talked about a "fundamental restructuring" of North American manufacturing and of world business, and has, through the two free trade agreements, invited that restructuring *into* Canada rather than attempting to protect Canada *from* it. The restructuring of Canadian industry has resulted in what business, government, and labour agree is the permanent loss of labour-intensive manufacturing jobs. The lowering or elimination of tariffs allow manufacturers to locate their production wherever in North America the available facilities, the skills of workers — and the level of wages they will accept — offer the best opportunities for profit. In Canada, new automated factories are built, but fewer workers are hired. The country's economic production increases at 2 to 3% per year, but the rate of unemployment remains stuck at around 11.5%. The economic forecasting group Informetrica predicts that employment will still be at least 10.5% in 1997. Citing University of California economist Paul Romer, David Crane writes in *The Toronto Star* "that we could see a growing polarization between rich and poor, with unskilled workers forced to accept continuing declines in their incomes due to competition from developing countries, while individuals with top education ... reap huge rewards."

All of the "user fee" and other economic proposals that politicians argue today are based on the assumption that wealth is for the most part distributed as a reward for physical, intellectual, or economic "work". This view holds that unemployment or depressed wages are an aberration created by unusual economic conditions, laziness or lack of training; that, as John Kenneth Galbraith expresses it, "the economic norm is high, if not quite full employment." It sees welfare and unemployment insurance either as stopgap measures used until the worker is re-employed or as ways of giving a minimum income to the unemployable.

The current wave of technological change, however, is in many cases making workers not unemployable but obsolete. High unemployment seems to have become not an aberration but a normal condition brought about permanently by technological change. The new automated factories are capable of producing enormous quantities of goods but are incapable of employing large numbers of workers. They thereby prevent those potential workers from becoming financially capable of buying the output of those automated factories. Such factories bring to many Canadian workers nothing less than the end of employment; to others they bring depressed wages as increasing numbers of unemployed workers compete for the available unskilled jobs. To society as a whole they thus bring a crippling limitation on employment's ability to perform as a mechanism by which the wealth generated by a country's enterprises is distributed to its citizens. To the present Canadian federal and provincial governments, they bring a seemingly endless deficit crisis — a crisis that is primarily a revenue crisis, caused by decreasing tax revenues as fewer and fewer Canadians earn taxable incomes. The situation moves Galbraith to consider the possibility of "an enduring underemployment equilibrium, of stability with high unemployment," and even to speculate that for the privileged members of society for whom low industrial wages and stable prices are advantages, "a recession is a tolerable, even pleasant thing."

"User fee," "cutback," "rollback," "deficit reduction," — all are catch words that have been selected by numerous politicians to define what they wish to present as the symptoms of this economic impasse. Their prominence in political debate, particularly in the Conservative leadership debate, to the exclusion of other potentially *useful* measures of dealing with the current recession and tax revenue crisis, reveals to the Canadian electorate how limited, and rigidly organized, is the scope of economic thinking presently offered by Canada's political leaders. Other possible economic measures — massive investments in education, for example, so that Canada might come to house such a disproportionate share of the world's wealth production that the country would be returned to nearly full, high-skilled employment; or imaginative ways of funding the lives of a large, permanently unemployed citizenry — are kept from serious consideration by the repeated and loud utterance of "user fees." In asking the leadership candidates not to talk of user fees, Campbell's cabinet colleague Bouchard substituted the word "imagination." "We have to develop with imagination," he said, "not to charge $5 to people who aren't able to pay." But "user fees" continued to be the term of choice for Tory candidates and delegates.

■

Along with "user fees" the second code word with which Kim Campbell chose to associate her name during the campaign was not anything like "imagination". It was "enemies." She announced, during the fourth leadership debate (see the quotation that began this chapter) that as prime minister she would campaign against "the enemies" of Canadians who tried to delude them into thinking "that debts and deficits are not a problem." In terms of the language of British Columbia politics (this debate took place in Vancouver), long polarized by Social Credit Red-baiting hyperbole, the use of this word was a lamentably too-familiar ploy of political rhetoric. It indicated in one breath the rigidities and intolerances common in the politics of Campbell's Socred past. In the United States' two-party system, the word would fit easily into the tradition of right-wing debate from Estes Kefauver, through Barry Goldwater, Shirley Temple Black, Richard Nixon, Anita Bryant, and Ronald Reagan. In these instances "enemies" is part of the vocabulary of evangelical, authoritarian certainty: Our opinions are right; yours, necessarily the enemies', are at the least metaphorically — treasonous. But Vancouver was not, in 1993 at least, the United States. The debate did occur in British Columbia, but was conducted within the language and practices of Canadian federal politics, not those of B.C. Thus the other candidates, all less familiar with the tenor of B.C. politics, expressed shock at Campbell's word choice. In the British parliamentary system, the word "enemy" is an affront: the opposition parties are "her majesty's loyal opposition"; their opposition is viewed as part of a critical process necessary to create good law. Jean Charest made his objections on such parliamentary grounds: "People who don't agree with our ideas are as Canadian as we are."

But the real potential problem for the Tories was that the word "enemy" removed the fuzziness of their position, which Charest himself had jestingly described to Turner earlier in the debate: "User fees if necessary but not necessarily user fees." It threatened to reveal as Tory enemies not only the opposition parties but the economically disadvantaged whom Canadian social programmes were designed to aid. If the users of social programmes are seen to be Tory enemies, "user fees" come to be understood as what Tory critics have always said they were: weapons against the poor. And the Campbell-led Tories themselves are self-portrayed as the enemies of those they would charge user fees.

Campbell quickly attempted to contain the effects of her "enemies" remark. She pointed out that she had qualified it as quickly as she had said it, arguing that "as soon as it was out of my mouth, I realized I had used a stronger word than I had meant to use ... I certainly wouldn't mean to offend anyone." But in a sophisticated society in which even many of the least educated understand the concept of the "Freudian slip," Campbell's apology served mainly to confirm her original statement. What slips out of one's mouth in a moment of stress — as too many domestic disputants have learned to their chagrin — is more often what one "means" than otherwise. "Enemies" had become one of the user fees attached to the "Campbell" candidacy. Some hours later, some Alberta journalists were even speculating that "enemies" had not been a slip at all, but a deliberate courting of right-wing Tory delegates.

Photo: Canapress

CHAPTER IX

Boys Will Be Boys

> When he told me [that she would be appointed Minister of Defence], I probably said 'Holy Cow, Prime Minister, Leapin' Lizards, Daddy Warbucks.' (Kim Campbell, quoted in *Maclean's*, 18 January 1993)

Early on the morning of May 17 I was woken as usual by CBC-AM on my clock radio. The music being played was a contemporary recording of "Shake, Rattle, and Roll," one of the "classic" rock 'n roll songs of the early 1950s, in which a male singer launches a vitriolic attack on his female partner for her passivity, failure to dress well for him, and neglecting to cook his breakfast. The title demands that she shape up — "shake, rattle, and roll" — because the singer is, in more than one way, "a hungry man." In my sleepiness I was surprised. Why was the female host of the show playing such a blatantly sexist song? Why had it been re-recorded? I was struck by the irony that when I'd been a teenager in the 1950s, the Bill Haley and his Comets version of the song, like most Bill Haley recordings, had seemed to be on a CBC blacklist. But now the Ontario regional CBC station was playing the song not as an interesting artifact, but as a "new" musical interpretation.

The following morning the same station woke me with news that in an interview with Peter Newman, published in part in *The Toronto Star*, Kim Campbell had said that people who don't join political parties have no right to criticize politicians, and that she had earlier in her life become an Anglican "as a way of warding off the evil demons of the papacy." The tone of the announcement implied that she had seriously and abruptly damaged her candidacy. I went across the street to the neighbourhood corner store to buy a copy of the *Star*, muttering to myself about how a supposedly intelligent woman like Campbell could let herself say such things. The *Star* article, "Campbell slams critics for 'apathy'," by Patrick Doyle, contained very little more information, except that the full interview had been published in *Vancouver Magazine*, that Campbell claimed to speak fluent Yiddish, that she'd said she wouldn't want to win the leadership like Joe Clark, "just 'because he was the least-hated candidate in the coliseum'," and that she had called those who criticize politicians without joining political parties themselves "condescending SOBs" — and added "To hell with them."

A few hours later I obtained the full text of Newman's article/interview from Vancouver by fax. It was a curious piece, not really an interview so much as an article about a three-hour luncheon interview, into which numerous quotations from the interview had been spliced. Its title, "Citizen Kim," flashed a warning sign that oddly seemed to refer to no specific point in the interview. This title appeared to link "Campbell" to Orson Welles' film treatment, *Citizen Kane*, of the life of publisher-politician William Randolph Hearst. The film had profiled the life of a man of wealth and privilege, but who lacked deep understanding of either people or politics; he had prospered through sensationalist journalism and outspoken opinions, but had failed in his search for high public office and had ended his life in personal disappointment. He had claimed, like Kim Campbell, to have been interested in public service rather than power. Welles had himself described Kane as someone who "sets himself up against the law, against the entire tradition of liberal civilization" (Cowie 32). Yet Newman's article made no further reference to *Citizen Kane*.

A second oddity in the article was a repeated gap between Newman's comments about Campbell and the quotations he supplied. "Campbell has a strong and definable ideology," he remarked in his second paragraph, but offered no examples of what this ideology might be. A page later he remarked that "Campbell was sounding so stone-certain about the boundaries of her aspirations and beliefs that I asked her to get up and sing Frank Sinatra's version of *My Way*." Yet the remarks he had quoted — that she would like to "be a prime minister on [her] own terms," that she would like to be selected leader "for who I am" rather than because "we've got to have a woman ... [t]hat's what they did in the NDP" — sounded more firm and partisan than narcissistic. Perhaps there were elements in the interview Newman was not supplying, or even quotations he was suppressing.

As for the remarks attributed to Campbell in the interview, by the CBC and the *Toronto Star*, these were not spoken precisely as they had represented them. Her comment on Clark's victory as someone "least-hated" was phrased not as an attack on him but as an observation that such a victory would make governing "very difficult." Her talk about "the evil demons of the papacy" was an ironic, self-mocking phrase within an amusing account of her enrollment, when twelve years old, in a convent school: "I got confirmed as an Anglican the year I was [there], I suppose as a way of warding off the evil demons of the papacy or whatever. But I have a lot of respect for the spiritual principles." Only the concluding sentences of the 9-page article/interview had the unequivocally strong, ungenerous language that the *Star* and the CBC had cited. And even here, it was hard to tell exactly whom Campbell was attacking.

> "I don't believe that democratic institutions run on autopilot," is Campbell's parting shot. "The thing that infuriates me is apathy. People who boast about how they've never been involved in a political party. Who do they think is working to keep this society intact so they can have the luxury of sitting back and being such condescending SOBs? To hell with them."

Was she really asking that people be made to join political parties before being allowed to make political comments? Not necessarily, although that meaning also wasn't excluded. Was the word "boast" present in the passage to intensify the effect or to restrict the passage's application only to those who boasted about not joining political parties? The passage opened by purporting to defend "democratic institutions" and seemed to end with a condemnation of the democratic right to abstain. Those who declined to join a party were "SOBs" — sons of bitches, illegitimate offspring, or, in political terms, illegitimate citizens. They were to be consigned "to hell," where in religion illegitimate souls are sent. The equivalent political hell would be disenfranchisement, the fate of a non-citizen.

But why was Newman calling this her "parting shot"? What similarly extravagant and exclusionary shots had he not reported?

■

A connection between the ominous language of Campbell's last six words in the Newman-Campbell interview and the plight of a woman who was commanded to go out into that kitchen and rattle those pots and pans would probably not have struck me most days. I had spent some time the day before, however, reflecting on "Shake, Rattle, and Roll," recalling that it hadn't originally been a "Bill Haley" song, although that was how white kids like myself experienced it, but had begun as a black-American one — a black community hit sung by the legendary rhythm-and-blues and "shout" singer Joe Turner. Its deplorable misogyny was at least understandable as a "kick-the-cat" reflex of black males who themselves were being ruthlessly abused by a dominant white culture. But why had it become so popular in white culture? Today there seems to be a parallel to this earlier adoption by whites of black music into white culture: witness the popularity of Afro-American rap music — with its even more extravagant expressions of anger, race hatred, and misogyny — among white audiences. White rap performers, like the Canadian "Snow," are even following in the 1950s footsteps of white rock 'n rollers like Haley and Presley in imitating black emotions and attitudes for white listeners. Why is this 1950s phenomenon repeating itself in the 1990s?

The answer, of course, is that misogyny and exploitation, together with the political, economic, and emotional disenfranchisement that accompany it, have never required the exploiter to be himself a member of an abused group. Even white journalists and politicians are permitted to participate. Misogyny and exploitation are fuelled just as efficiently by the enjoyment of power as by suffering and abuse, regardless of race. And women as well as men can "buy into" both the misogyny and the abuse. In fact most of the fans who screamed deliriously when Elvis sang contemptuously to his beloved that she was nothing but a hound dog, crying all the time, were young women — unthinkingly accepting a view of themselves as weak, passive, easily depressed, parasitical on men, *and* unthinkingly rewarding the appropriation of a black musical idiom. The American feminist critic Annette Kolodny has described this acceptance of misogyny as showing how a male-dominated culture teaches women to have "self-hatred" — to hate themselves for not being more like men. But self-hatred isn't only expressed by the hero worship of men who sing songs that celebrate woman-abuse, or by the passive-aggressive forgetting to go to the kitchen and rattle pots and pans. It is obliquely expressed also by a woman broadcaster who in 1993 can give an "updated" performance of "Shake, Rattle, and Roll" airtime. It is expressed in a different way by a woman who utters phrases like "condescending SOBs" and "to hell with them." Such phrases are not only marked in our culture as the locker-room and board-room language of men. They are also phrases, "SOB" transparently so, that operate directly against the interests of women, who only became enfranchised in all parts of Canada in 1940. Had it been other comments like this that had caused Newman to make his *Citizen Kane* connection, and his remarks about Campbell's being ideological and "stone-certain"? And lo, here in the middle of the interview was Kim Campbell speaking admiringly of the black-derived music of Bill Haley and his Comets. "Her tastes are varied," Newman diplomatically began.

> She's the only person I ever met who could intelligently diagnose Bill Haley & The Comets. ("He was really on the cusp, still heavy on the saxophone but the brass are beginning to decline, and a lot of his music is really exciting because it was so experimental.")

Intelligent formal diagnosis, perhaps. But no awareness of the enormous social issues that had been at stake in Haley's music.

■

For the next week debate raged in Canadian newspapers over whether the CBC and the *Star* had dealt fairly with the Newman interview. Word was passed that Jean Charest staffers, unsuccessful in bringing the interview to national attention in the two weeks following its publication, had circulated selectively marked excerpts of it to Ottawa journalists the day before the *Star* publication. The *Globe* ran side-by-side comparisons of the *Vancouver Magazine,* CBC, and *Star* texts, under the headline "Just what was (and wasn't) said." In a column entitled "Misrepresenting Kim Campbell," *Globe* columnist Michael Valpy attempted to explain Campbell's remarks by contextualizing them with the comment that British Columbia is "less restrained by notions of propriety" than any other part of the country. "Campbell's frankness manipulated by news media" announced a column by Ken MacQueen in the *London Free Press*. The *Star* ombudsman, Don Sellar, however, found its reporting to be a "better job" than Newman's "upbeat and breezy magazine article." Letters to the *Star* mostly agreed with Sellars, appearing under titles like "Exceeuuuuse me, to hell with her" and "A reflection of Kim's conceit." The *Globe* also published a few additional parts of the interview that Newman had published in a privately-circulated business newsletter, with rather more negative and Citizen Kane-like comments about "Campbell" than he had made in *Vancouver Magazine.*

> She had never held an economic portfolio and seems uninterested in this vital aspect of her mandate.
>
> ... [it is] an unparalleled advantage for a prime minister to have a feel for the country he or she hopes to govern, and to possess an intimate knowledge of his or her party through which governance will be exercised. Kim Campbell has demonstrated neither. (Howard, "Campbell stands up for PM")

This extended debate, however, in looking for Truth and verbal accuracy was asking the wrong questions. It was not the literal meaning of Campbell's words that was going to determine what she had "said"; it was the social meanings carried by the language — the vocabulary and discourse — she had employed. Strictly speaking, the CBC and the *Star* had indeed misrepresented her words by taking them, as some critics noted, "out of context." But the words themselves — "evil demons," "SOBs," "to hell" — had unsettled people because they affiliated "Campbell" with a vocabulary of totalitarian intolerance, a vocabulary to which her "enemies" remark a few weeks earlier had also linked her. Like that word, these additional ones — blurted out in the pleasure and sociability of a luncheon — appeared to be "Freudian slips," more reliable signs of how she perceived the world than any number of carefully chosen phrases might be. Valpy's suggestion about context was technically correct — her words might not seem out of place to her "home audience." They might also, he could have added, not seem out of place in quite a number of politically less tolerant countries. But Campbell was seeking office in a national Canadian context. Some British Columbians might tolerate politicians who could conceive of saying "to hell" to some of their fellow citizens, but Canadians elsewhere might very well not.

■

> ... [M]y approach always has been to be who I am, to articulate my vision and run up my flag and see if anybody salutes. (Campbell, in Newman)

I am aware as I write this, however, that some readers might well suspect another misogynist aspect to the Newman interview and its aftermath beyond the one I am suggesting here: to what extent was the negative reaction to it — like the lyrics of "Shake, Rattle, and Roll," or like Campbell's own use of violent, masculine, autocratic, or military imagery throughout the interview — an attack on women? There had been a symbolic sense of "attack the woman" visible throughout the Tory leadership campaign as five "hungry men" squared off in each debate against one front-running woman. Violence against her had been hinted at in many of the headlines — for instance, the *Globe*'s "Campbell under gun in Calgary" (April 26), and "Charest comes out swinging" (May 14). In the case of the interview itself, an argument could be made that Campbell was being attacked for not talking more kindly — like a woman "should" — or was being singled out for scrutiny while Charest was not. Such feminist claims are made frequently when the "unkind" woman under attack is a poet or novelist, or even a woman politician speaking in defence of women's interests.

It is quite possible that the general reason such arguments were not publically suggested was that feminist leaders, as we'll see in the next chapter, had already defined Campbell as a person who aspired to lead a party that in general works against women's interests. It is also quite possible that the vocabulary of authoritarianism and intolerance Campbell had associated herself with may have appeared to most men and women to be a language that was in no one's interest — with the exception of those already in positions of authority and power.

One of the first party events for the Conservative leadership candidates, in fact, had shown the public a glimpse of the intolerances that characterized factions of the party that Campbell was seeking to impress and lead. The event was the Alberta Progressive Conservative Party annual convention, held in Edmonton, April 3 and 4. News reports suggested that Campbell's rival Jean Charest had been very comfortable there, but that she herself had seemed less relaxed. The *Globe* story, by Miro Cernetig, reported that Charest

> gave a folksy speech, punctuated with jokes, that built on his image as a Quebec federalist, and spent hours shaking hands with delegates.
>
> Defence Minister Kim Campbell displayed her intense quick-paced speaking style and was kept to a carefully timed itinerary by her entourage.

Later in the article, some possible reasons for Charest's relatively greater sense of comfort became apparent. There had been some "behind the scenes attacks on Ms. Campbell," that had been "aimed at her reputation as being overly elitist, and a perception that she is not the sort of woman the party's right wing is comfortable with." The article quoted one of the delegates, a Ken Chapman, to have said that "Ms. Campbell's urban roots, her two failed marriages and her academic style are hurting her in some corners.... It's not about whether a woman can do the job," Chapman was supposed to have said, but "whether that kind of woman can do the job." Later it quoted a party official to have said that Campbell could not win a majority of delegates in the province because "She's a woman and this is Alberta."

What "sort of woman" the party might find acceptable became evident the next day, after the candidates had left, and the Alberta party staged a cabaret show for its own amusement. At that event, Premier Ralph Klein was reported by Miro Cernetig of the *Globe*, in an article entitled "Klein's PC's hardly PC," to have danced in a chorus line of cancan dancers, former Intergovernmental Affairs minister Jim Horsman to have played the part of an effeminate gay waiter in an openly homophobic skit, and Minister of Culture Dianne Mirosh to have mimicked Mae West in coyly asking a workman "Is that a hammer in your pocket or are you just glad to see me?"

By an odd coincidence — or perhaps through Peter Newman's mischievousness — the Newman interview linked itself directly to that cabaret scene, and created the possibility that Campbell might not have been as out of place among Alberta Tories as Cernetig reported. Perhaps she was even their "sort of woman." The interview quoted her as having "privately parodied" her much vaunted pro-feminist gun-control legislation in the same unfeminist Mae West line that Mirosh had used: "Say, fella, is that a prohibited weapon with a barrel length of less than 18 inches, possession of which is grandfathered by those who satisfy the requirement of being a genuine gun collector on or before October 1, 1992, in your pocket, or are you just glad to see me?" As in the case of most of Campbell's provocative remarks, Newman had no comment to make about it. But its ambiguous humour — which could be read as making fun of the restrictions or as mocking the amount of protection they offered women — at the very least called into question, one way or another, Campbell's commitment to a bill on which part of her social justice reputation rested.

■

Meanwhile another "sort of woman" was also giving some members of the Conservative party a different kind of difficulty. This was Sunera Thobani, who in mid-April was named as the sole nominee for the June 5-7 election of the president of the National Action Committee for the Status of Women. Thobani is a Tanzanian immigrant of South Asian descent, and a doctoral student at Simon Fraser University. Her right to hold the position was promptly challenged in Parliament by Conservative MP John MacDougall, who misinformed the house that she was an illegal immigrant, and later explained that he believed the job should be held by a Canadian citizen. In a *Globe* article of May 10, "Heir to NAC stung by attack," reporter

Deborah Wilson wrote that Thobani had been "wounded" by MacDougall's charges, and that other NAC members, who believed the charges to be racist and anti-feminist, had asked the Prime Minister to discipline him. Wilson, however, suggested that Thobani was being naïve, that her reaction suggested "an unfamiliarity with the casual brutality of national politics, and extreme discomfort with the everyday intrusions of the mainstream news media." Wilson's remarks acted to defend the way things are done — the practices of national politics and the "everyday" ones of her own profession — even though she recognized that at least the first of these is "brutal."

In *The Toronto Star* a few days later, long-time Conservative Dalton Camp also commented on the Thobani controversy, in a column entitled "In tussle of Thobani let's not forget legacy of NAC's rude jousting." Camp went even further than Wilson in defending what had happened as normal: "It is not at all unusual for our parliamentarians to say things that are untrue; we have, indeed, erected a political system rooted in the premise that our politicians may say anything that comes into their heads while speaking in our legislatures." He was surprised that Thobani had taken MacDougall seriously. In effect, Camp and Deborah Wilson had enlarged MacDougall's attack on Thobani. To MacDougall's charges that as a recent immigrant she could not adequately represent Canadian women, they had added the accusation that her response to MacDougall showed that she didn't understand the implicitly male-dominated rough-and-tumble world of Canadian politics.

What links the Thobani issue to the Alberta Tory conventions is the untroubled acceptance in both cases of both political and verbal violence, not just against women but against other Canadians. In the Alberta context, a heterosexual male is the norm. A woman candidate, particularly if the wrong "sort of woman," is likely to be unacceptable; a homosexual — defined in Horsman's wrist-flipping gestures as female — is both the wrong sort of man and the wrong "sort of woman," and the legitimate open target of outright parody and ridicule. In the Thobani case, MacDougall has found her too to be the wrong sort of woman. In turn, Deborah Wilson has found his "brutality" routine and therefore acceptable. Camp has found MacDougall's remarks routine and therefore forgettable. Thobani and her women defenders, however, have a different perspective. The brutality should not be accepted because it is normal, but repudiated because it is discriminatory, an abuse of the politically weak by the powerful. Thobani in her explanation of the event parallels it to her mother's being struck by an ice-packed snowball thrown by a young man in a truck. Normality is not to be accepted, she suggests, but revised.

■

> What it comes down to in a circumstance of this nature is whether you would have any support from senior female members of the cabinet to make it clear that this would be a race about substance and ideas and not an old-boys gang-up. (Hugh Segal, declining to be a candidate, 8 April 1993, quoted in Winsor, 9 April 1993)

This question, posed by Hugh Segal in announcing that he would not accept a party draft to enter the leadership race, remained despite his announcement, a major element in the Tory race. The question had, in effect, two parts. The overt one was whether the party, with the help of the media, and with or without Segal, would "gang-up" on Campbell and attempt to prevent her victory. The more hidden one was whether the system of Canadian politics — its language of "casual brutality" and violence, its "little boy's games" (Campbell's own description of the five debates) of one-upmanship, its dependency for funding on the male-dominated arenas of big-business and big-lobbying — had long ago acted to make "Kim Campbell" into an anger-venting politician — Sheila Copps' "Mulroney in skirts."

The first question seemed initially to disappear with the phantom Segal and Clark candidacies, but re-surfaced emphatically in the last week of the campaign when it appeared that Charest had a genuine chance of winning. Charest supporters began to praise him in a vocabulary carefully selected to offer contrasts to a "Kim Campbell" whose past was varied and eccentric, and whose public pronouncements had often been blunt, dramatic or overstated. Joe Clark was among the first of these supporters, repeatedly emphasizing during his June 7 endorsement of Charest that he perceived him to be "calm" in a crisis. Clark's wife, Maureen McTeer, joined him, declaring that she preferred Charest because he was "stable." In each case, the implication was that Kim Campbell might not be "calm" or "stable" (see Speirs, "Campbell unfazed as Clark backs Charest"). On June 9, in offering editorial support to Charest, *The Globe and Mail* made a similar but more clear distinction in praising Charest for "forthrightness," for an ability to "assert legitimate federal authority," and for having "less complexity...: what you see is more or less what you get," while criticizing Campbell for "brittleness," "defensiveness," and "unpredictability" ("On balance, Jean Charest"). The sexist stereotypes that had been hinted at by Clark and McTeer were here in the open: Charest was masculinely forthright and straightforward; Campbell was one of those complicated women men can never understand or predict.

On the same day, the "gang-up" feared by Segal gathered momentum when Tory MP Terry Clifford endorsed

Charest over Campbell because Charest had a family. "I think that clearly, somebody who has a family — that they have to look after and bring up — has got a commitment to other people who have families," he told reporters at a news conference ("Clifford raises marital status as campaign issue"). His views were quickly echoed by Southam columnist Rory Leishman in an article titled "Charest's qualities make him best choice," where he wrote "Instead of cosying up to groups like NAC, the leader of the Progressive Conservative party would do better to concentrate on winning over the great majority of Canadians — men and women, who cherish the natural family — husband, wife and children." By a strange coincidence, all these loaded remarks were made during a week that also saw the announcement that British Columbia MLA Judy Tyabji had lost a bid for custody of her children because a male judge had been persuaded that the busy life of an elected politician made her a less fit parent. It was Robert Mason Lee of *The Vancouver Sun* who slyly observed the "Sophie's choice" contrast between Tyabji's and Campbell's situations: "If you hold public office then you are unfit to have children, but if you do not have children, then you are unfit to hold public office."

However, given Campbell's convention victory, the second question raised by Segal's remarks — of whether the persistent and systemic violence of the Canadian political system, together with its tight ties to male power centres like the financial and legal communities, had predefined "Campbell," lingered on. Campbell had already demonstrated a continuing attraction to two of the most anti-woman of Canadian political parties. As justice minister, she had appeared to bend to rural gun-control opponents in responding to the call for tighter weapons restrictions that followed the University of Montreal killings. But she had also continued to define herself as a feminist, and in speeches to women's groups had offered perceptive and personal analyses of the relationships between women and power. In launching her campaign, she had called for a greater openness in government in order to counter what she called a growing "political cynicism" among Canadians "about the political process as a whole." Such an openness could come about only by diminishing the power that male-dominated institutions — the cabinet, the House of Commons, the Bank of Canada, the legal and banking professions, the Canadian Manufacturers Association, the lobbyists for large corporations — enjoy in our political system, and by shifting power toward institutions in which women's roughly 52% share of the population is more accurately represented. She had also called on her Prime Minister not to fill vacant Senate seats before the next election. Again the potential losers in such a policy would be mainly men, and the losing social groups would be politicians and business. The two Senate appointments announced by Mulroney in unwitting answer to Campbell later that day were former Alberta MLA Ron Ghitter, federal campaign manager for the Conservatives in that province, and Winnipeg businessman Terrance Stratton, federal Tory campaign manager in 1988 for Manitoba.

In one of her first policy speeches, on April 19, Campbell called for reform of lobbying practices. She suggested that lobbyists who had financially supported or worked for politicians, such as herself and other leadership candidates, should be required to reveal the names of the politicians they supported. She proposed also that lobbyists be required to reveal specifically whom they are attempting to influence, who they are employed by, and what policies they are trying to achieve. Again, because of the present enormous overrepresentation of men among Canadian federal politicians, cabinet ministers, and high-level party organizers, and because lobbyists are almost all retired politicians, high-level civil servants, or political workers, such a policy would disadvantage mostly men and the political practices that assure the continuing disproportionate influence of men on Canadian public policy. It would also disadvantage the commercial and financial institutions that are the most frequent employers of lobbyists, and the most active supporters of the Conservative party.

Campbell's difficulty here is a classic instance of conflict of interest — not the kind of conflict of financial interest that we attempt to require politicians to disclose, but a more general conflict of interests and values. Campbell's gender interests are those of women; she works, as she told a convention of women journalists, to change a world in which "physically, women do not correspond with ... ideas of what a politician is." Her regional interest is British Columbia, far from Bay Street and the Ottawa lobbyists. Her class interests began in the lower middle-class world of her young lawyer-father, and have slowly moved into the upper middle-class ones of the academy and professional politics. But her professional interests lie in the Conservative party, with its hegemony of male MPs, organizers, and corporate and financial backers. Her personal interests within that party rest largely with Ottawa and Bay Street lobbyists — as the *Globe*'s Ross Howard listed them, "top gun William Neville, Michael Coates, Peter Burn, Sharon Andrews and pollster David Crapper of Hill and Knowlton; Jennifer Lynch of Lang, Michener; Nigel Wright of Davies, Ward, Beck; Jim Everson and Jill Maase of S.A. Murray Consulting; Nancy Jamieson; Libby Burnham of Borden and Eliot; Paul Curley of Advance Planning; Jon Johnson and James Crossland of Government Policy Consultants, and James MacEachern of Government Strategies Corp, to name a few." One may be forgiven, I think, if one suspects after reading such a list that the work of these people on the Campbell campaign may not have come without cost to their companies, and that as well as being beholden to the individuals, "Campbell" herself has been becoming day by day more beholden to the very firms her lobbyist proposals would disadvantage.

Of even more concern is the question of how much phrases like "condescending SOBs" suggest that "Kim Campbell" is really very at ease with and tolerant of both the casual brutality of "normal," male-dominated Canadian politics and the intermittent flashes of intolerance among Tories. Do such phrases suggest that she would increase rather than decrease social intolerance? The "political cynicism" among "Canadians as a whole" she vowed, in her campaign-launching speech to address, has in fact been produced by precisely this kind of casually brutal, exaggerated rhetoric, coupled with casually brutal reversals of policy. If Canadians are not taking part in party politics, and are "cynical" about the political process, it is because of politicians who promise to curtail lobbying and then make themselves beholden to lobbyists. It is because of politicians like Brian Mulroney who condemned patronage appointments and then loaded the Senate with superannuated Tories in order to gain passage for the GST; who "rolled the dice" on Canada's constitution and then branded as "enemies" Canadians who would not roll with him; who declared social programmes a "sacred trust" and then proposed curtailment of the old age pension. Yet in the interview in which Campbell labels those disaffected by party politics "condescending SOBs" she also declares "enormous respect" for Mulroney." Blaming the victim, the poor "SOB," for his own disaffection, is unfortunately a classic ploy of totalitarian thought. The next step is, predictably, "to hell."

■

Kim Campbell's fanciful and charming reconstruction of her reaction to being appointed minister of defence — "Holy Cow, Prime Minister, Leapin' Lizards, Daddy Warbucks — captures an extraordinary amount of the meanings that her name now carries with it. Like the "enemies of Canadians," and "condescending SOBs" remarks, it appears to be a piece of language that has slipped uncensored from her mouth, and therefore reflects her most usual way of viewing herself and events. Her reconstruction shows her to be impetuous, endearing, apparently genuinely delighted with her own success. But her success seems — even to herself — like that of a small child in an authoritarian and male-dominated world. Her hero, the Mulroney for whom she claims such "enormous respect," is "Daddy Warbucks," the rigidly right-wing entrepreneur of the equally right-wing U.S. comic strip *Little Orphan Annie*. She is again a little redhead, a little *orphaned* redhead, struggling for recognition, legitimacy, and approval in a violent, authoritarian, and intolerant society. Real power to change her life lies with men with guns and with the male institutions which Little Orphan Annie's "Daddy Warbucks" represented — patriarchy, the military, and the military's close partner, high finance. In the imagination of a woman who sees herself, even jestingly, as Little Orphan Annie to Mulroney's Daddy Warbucks, there could indeed be numerous guns, enemies, and SOBs.

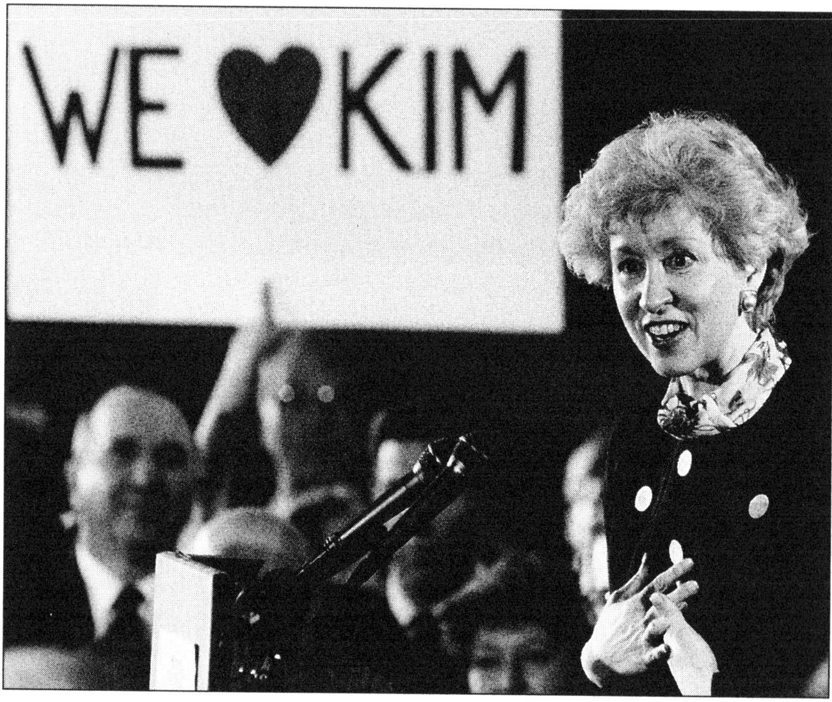

Photo: Canapress

CHAPTER X
Not Liking Kim

> Anytime you have a blonde with bare shoulders in March in the middle of a recession, the political libido has to bounce. (Allan Fotheringham)

> Social Credit was a valuable political instrument, and I wanted to be a part of redefining it. (Kim Campbell, Newman interview)

At the Conservative Party's five leadership debates, there were two disturbances within the conventional field of Canadian political imagery. One was indeed Campbell's blonde hair, her variable dress, among the five sombrely suited men. The second was John Long, barely articulate in either language, the only candidate not a Member of Parliament, who was introduced on each occasion as a "businessman." While the other five candidates offered views and fielded questions on numerous issues — economics, regional development, social programmes, the environment, defence, education — Long had a view on only one issue, and attempted to offer this no matter what question he was asked. This issue was monetary policy. He spoke incoherently but predictably about his membership in the national Social Credit party twenty years ago, about ruinously high interest rates, exploitation by "big finance," "bank deposit money," and legislation that would require the Bank of Canada to make low-interest loans to Canadian small businesses, and to loan the government money to pay off the national debt. In none of the debates did the other candidates talk about these economic proposals, but waited with expressionless faces for his seemingly irrelevant remarks to finish. The delegates offered him minimally polite applause, and smiled discreetly to each other at his increasingly predictable incoherence and repetitiveness.

In his written responses to SouthamStar's "The candidates speak on the issues," Long was only slightly more coherent. He advocated "monetary reform" to reduce the deficit, and "a derivative tax on trading of securities and a wealth tax ... which would be opposed by big finance but it is time we started to run this country for the benefits of Canadians," and "[m]assive spending by the Bank of Canada on infrastructure housing and education." As Long's reminder of his Social Credit past hinted to the delegates, these policies were fragments of Social Credit policies that had circulated in Canada since the Aberhart government in Alberta in 1936, and that had over the years become little-understood scraps of both conservative and populist rhetoric.

The silence with which the other candidates greeted Long's remarks was not surprising. The Progressive Conservative party's relationship to Social Credit is in many ways as embarrassing and potentially problematical for it as was John Long's awkward presence on the leadership stage. In several parts of Canada — British Columbia, Alberta, and rural Quebec — varieties of Social Credit and the Conservative party have served the same constituencies. British Columbia's Social Credit party was founded by a disaffected Conservative. For many decades in both B.C. and Alberta, the party represented in provincial political contestation the ideological position occupied in all the other provinces by a Conservative party. In Alberta the fall and rise of the provincial Conservatives mirrored the rise and fall of the Socreds. Politicians moved easily, like Bennett, between the two provincial parties, or like Kim Campbell, easily between the provincial Social Credit party and the federal Conservatives.

Historically, Social Credit began as a set of economic theories offered early in this century by the English engineer, Major C.H. Douglas. Douglas' theories rested on his perception that the wages and salaries paid to produce an object were never sufficient for the workers to purchase the object they produced. The selling price contained not only their wages (which Douglas called "A") but also bank charges and the cost of raw materials (which he called "B"). Unless some way could be found to distribute to workers enough additional money so that their total income equalled "A plus B," the worker would live in poverty and the nation's economy would be glutted with unsold goods.

Douglas' explanation for the persistence of this state of affairs was that it benefitted bankers and financiers who, in most cases, could collect the bank charges and interest payments they levied. Its worst effects were the limitations it placed on individual workers, restricting their freedom of enjoyment and purchase. The solutions were threefold. One was state regulation of credit, even to the extent of the state participating in the banking system, so that the cost of "B" could be controlled and reduced. A second was the establishment of a state commission to set a "Just Price" for goods, a price that would be equal not to the cost of production but to the goods' present cost of replacement. The Just Price, he theorized, would decline as productivity and mechanization rose, enabling workers, whose wages had been lower than the original cost of production, to afford to buy the same objects that were now priced at the current cost of production. It would also reward workers and employers for increased productivity, fulfilling his belief that the free individual should be rewarded for effort and encouraged to make the most use of abilities. A third solution was to distribute to all citizens a "National Dividend," based on the notion that both natural resources and factory installations are common "Cultural Heritage," whose value should be kept out of the hands of bankers. The Cultural Heritage was real wealth, and the state's issuance of the National Dividend as a social "credit" would ensure the use and circulation of this wealth by all individuals.

Although some elements in this programme may sound socialist, particularly the notion of "Cultural Heritage," Douglas vigorously opposed socialists and Marxists because of what he perceived as their need to direct and control the lives of individuals through a large state bureaucracy. While Douglas in some of his writings approved of state confiscation of such things as railways, canals, and factories, because these enhanced the ability of the individual to work and had already been paid for communally by purchases of their products and services, he was opposed to a large state bureaucracy and saw most of his economic measures as being largely self-regulating.

If, overall, Douglas' programme seems incoherent, it may be because — as John Finlay suggests — he was an "intuitive" thinker who rarely "managed to get down on paper exactly what he wanted to say." Finlay notes that many of his writings appear "at best bizarre," and quotes statements like "The Foreign Office is the home of the Roman Catholic interest and the Treasury that of the Jewish" (96); or another that explains that economic problems are "a very deeply laid and well considered plot of enslaving the industrial world to the German-American-Jewish financiers" (103).

Douglas' proposals reflect very specific understandings

of economic relationships and operate to the advantage of very specific interest groups within a society. Yet when commentators on Canadian politics suggest, often correctly, that there is very little connection between Major Douglas' idiosyncratic proposals and the particular policies of Canadian Social Credit parties, they tend to overlook these underlying assumptions and interests. One crucial understanding of Douglas' ideology is that each citizen is an individual, an entrepreneur, and not a member of a group, class, or union. Group membership is a constraint upon individual talent and freedom. Douglas finds social formations which intrude upon individuality, whether these be labour unions or large financial cartels, to be potential disturbances to his general theory. Almost all Social Credit movements have followed Douglas in being dogmatically anti-Marxist and suspicious of both John Long's "big finance" and trade unionism. A second understanding is that monetary policy should benefit the worker, the small businessman, and the general citizenry. Low interest rates and regulated prices are to keep money in circulation so that goods can be readily sold. A third understanding implicit within his theories, although not directly addressed, is the continuing enrichment of those who can accumulate, not money, which is regulated, but material goods — the things a Douglas economy values above all else and encourages its citizens to produce, sell, and consume. A fourth is the Douglas Social Credit's narrowly focussed materialism: all political effort is directed at economic development. There is no consideration of "culture" as a humanistic or artistic rather than an economic activity. It is a politics that would indeed tax books.

The naïveté in Douglas' theories — that they could be practised within a world economy conducted on different lines; that financiers might not take their money to regions where they were less regulated; that the issuance of the social "credit" would not cause inflation; that individuals would feel safe accumulating goods and property in a society that permitted some forms of state confiscation; that his economy would always expand and allow a Just Price that was lower than the original cost of production — has indeed prevented the specifics of his policies from being treated seriously in Canada, let alone implemented. Moreover, his own harsh rhetoric against bankers and Jews, and the linking of Social Credit by many thinkers — Ezra Pound most conspicuously among them — to German and Italian fascism, which similarly viewed moneylending as a social vice and opposed Marxism with even more dogmatic vigour, has also tended to discredit it.

As a way of thinking about society, and as a way of using language to create verbal images of society, however, Canadian Social Credit cannot be considered to be unconnected from its Major Douglas past. Social Credit in Canada has been primarily the party of small business and small landowners, and has been located in regions of the country historically remote from both international "big finance" and concentrations of organized labour. Within those regions it has tended to be unpopular in large urban centres but popular in rural areas, where there is often proportionally greater self-employment. Social Credit's first Canadian leader, William "Bible Bill" Aberhart, was an entrepreneurial evangelist, whose independent and charismatic practices led him to break with established churches and found his own sect, The Bible Institute Baptist Church. Its second important leader, W.A.C. Bennett, was a Kelowna, B.C., hardware merchant. The history of British Columbia Social Credit reflects both Major Douglas' suspicion of big business and his anti-Marxism. Banks and big business were suspected by the party of operating in the interests in Central Canadians, or in the interests of their shareholders, and against those of

"British Columbians." In cases in which companies appeared to be operating in flagrant conflict with state policy — the Black Ball ferry company in 1958, and the B.C. Electric Company in 1961 (both of which had appeared to be obstructing Social Credit's plans to open rural areas to entrepreneurial development) — they were to be nationalized. At the same time, lacking a Marxist opposition, Social Credit created one out of the CCF/NDP, depicting it in election after election as a "Red" tide of creeping socialism. It repeatedly resisted a view of the worker as part of a collective rather than as an individual, opposed "closed shop" union agreements, the right to strike, and anti-strikebreaking laws, and proposed "right to work" legislation. In the cultural sphere, Canadian Social Credit has tended to practise a pragmatic philistinism. It has founded universities to provide the trained graduates a growing economy needs, but founded no large arts councils and offered at best token encouragement to publishers, public galleries, and individual artists.

Kim Campbell's affiliation with Social Credit can in a sense be regarded as "natural" given the bipolar character of British Columbia's politics from 1952 to the present. What other party could a conservative B.C. politician who hoped to be elected have joined? But on the other hand, the effects of that political scene, and the effects of years of taking seriously the rhetoric of that party remain with her, as even Michael Valpy's defence of her "SOB" remarks hints: "Ms. Campbell candidly, as they say in the therapy trade, discloses — and in a very West Coast way." Her family background is the same self-employed small-business class that has provided the main constituency of Canadian Social Credit — her father a lawyer, her grandfathers, according to Newman, a dairy farmer and a dentist. Her first strong political opinions were vigorously anti-Marxist and anti-Soviet, acquired while married to the outspokenly right-wing Nathan Divinsky, and while studying under Sovietologist Leonard Schapiro at the London School of Economics; "[her] studies at LSE reinforced her conservative views. . . . Campbell emerged from [Schapiro's] influence with a loathing for leftist dogma . . ." (Fulton and Janigan). A few sentences before uttering her unfortunate "enemies" remark at the Vancouver debate, she invoked her British Columbian roots and chided her opponents for not having been equal to the rough-and-ready demands of British Columbia political language. In her words one could hear echoes not only of W.A.C Bennett's rhetoric, and of Mulroney's earlier use of "enemies," but also of the suspicious and hostile language of Major Douglas.

Moreover, Campbell's declaration to Peter Newman that "Social Credit was a valuable political instrument" has implications far beyond the most charitable reading one could give it — that Social Credit was a practical choice for a young B.C. politician cynically seeking an "instrument" through which to get elected. It is, after all, a statement made by a woman who has studied economics and political theory at advanced levels at one of the most sophisticated research institutions in the world. She knows both by study and personal experience what Social Credit can be a "political instrument" for, and what Canadian Social Credit has historically been an effective "instrument" in achieving: material prosperity for the self-employed middle and upper classes, a reduction in labour standards, ruthless exploitation and despoiling of natural resources to ensure industrial expansion, an anti-democratic restriction of political options through a right-left polarization of social debate, and a pervasive philistinism that places environmental, arts, and cultural values far below the goal of rewarding entrepreneurship. She knows, in short, that Social Credit has been an "instrument" for achieving a culture of temporary and shallow pleasures for the relatively wealthy. Her very choice of the word "instrument" to describe Social Credit to Newman shows her clear grasp of the party's pragmatism, materialism, and commitment to public manipulation. Her expanding her declaration by saying she had wanted "to be part of redefining" the Social Credit "instrument" is in this context at least a little frightening. Unless she is talking about subverting Social Credit, which seems extremely unlikely given her own enthusiastically conservative history on economic matters, it can only mean working toward a more *effective* Social Credit — more effective in glamourizing itself so that the public is seduced into supporting it, and thereby more effective in continuing the material enrichment of the prosperous — and the material, cultural, and environmental impoverishment of the rest of society.

■

The people who have appeared to be unhappy about the rising career of Kim Campbell, however, have included many more than just those who have opposed B.C. Social Credit or who have been shocked by the implications of its past and present policies and rhetoric. Feminists, NDP supporters, gay-rights activists, Liberals, Red Tories, far-right Tories, Bloc Québécois supporters, Reform Party supporters, the REAL Women — all have expressed their reservations and in some cases outright disapproval. Grumpy male chauvinists, like Allan Fotheringham, reduce Campbell to "bare shoulders," and her political appeal to mere displaced sexual energy. By conventional wisdom, her making unhappy so many people of so many different commitments would suggest she was a moderate, who cut compromises that made no one feel well-served. Such a theory has indeed been advanced as one of the things that is wrong with "Kim Campbell."

People who might have some reason to have personal reservations about her — her ex-husbands, her rivals in other parties, her rivals for the Tory leadership — have been among the least critical. Her ex-husbands have declined the invitations of journalists to be interviewed. Bill Vander Zalm, presently known mainly for having suffered the sting of Campbell's wit, has contented himself with remarking to *Maclean's* that in his Social Credit caucus "There used to be a joke: 'If it isn't Kim's idea, it probably isn't any good'." Her fellow leadership candidates made ironic allusions to her campaign slogan of "inclusiveness," and Jean Charest pointedly described himself as a person who wished to carry out policies rather than merely "be" prime minister. But all seemed to mute whatever criticisms they might have had of her. After Campbell's "enemies of Canadians" announcement, Charest — perhaps mindful of the wide range of views and interests the contemporary Conservative Party contains — charitably suggested it had been a mere "slip of the tongue."

Cartoonists have in general presented a more negative view. Most have exaggerated the length of her face, enlarged her nose, and set her eyes close together, giving her a pinched, ferret-like appearance. Nipper, in *The London Free Press,* portrayed on May 6 an erect, belligerent "Campbell" whose legs are invisible and who snarls "You know where I stand." Nease, also in the *Free Press,* on May 8 showed a "Campbell" head passing across the sky as a comet, with a child calling out below "Look mom, a falling star" — an apparent allusion to the *Maclean's* issue of January 18 that named her "a rising star." In a series of cartoons, Gable of *The Globe and Mail* depicted a "Kim Campbell" who is the driver of a powerful Indy-type racing car and who challenges a boyish Jean Charest and his tiny soapbox race car to a contest. In the April 17 cartoon, her enormous car had broken down and Charest was coasting past, saying "Welcome to the race." The general interpretation of "Kim Campbell" these cartoons gave was one of arrogance, meanness, and grandiose failure. Other cartoons portrayed her as the recipient of irrationally enthusiastic support. An April 18 cartoon by Corrigan of *The Toronto Star* showed Charest with his hand being raised in victory in the debating ring while a relaxed, unbruised, and happy "Campbell" sat below with her back to him, reading one of hundreds of papers and magazines that surrounded her with her own name in bold headlines. A cartoon by Hogan of the *Moncton Times-Transcript*, reprinted in *The Globe and Mail* on April 10, showed a solemn Hugh Segal, surrounded, even buffeted, by Campbell campaign signs, announcing that he would not be a leadership candidate. On the positive side, the message of all these cartoons was that Campbell was the only serious candidate for the leadership. The other candidates rarely appeared, except for Charest who was depicted as Campbell's foil — the little boy she would eventually zoom past, the naïve boxer who mistakes where the real contest is occurring.

Cartoons, of course, tend to rely for their humour on the creation of irony. They almost always create an ironic victim — someone who is unaware of what others can see, like the "Campbell" in the Nipper cartoon, unaware that her legs are invisible, or Charest in the Corrigan cartoon, unaware that though he has won the fight Campbell has received the admiring headlines; or someone whose expectations have been surprisingly disappointed. Sometimes they also portray a victor, as "Campbell" in the Corrigan depiction, and sometimes even a moral victor, as Charest seems to be momentarily in the Gable cartoon, as he drifts past "Campbell's" stalled racer. The ironic victim in the political cartoon is usually a politician already in power, portrayed as deserving a comeuppance. It is rarely an aspiring politician, unless the cartoonist wishes to portray him or her as unworthy of ascent. What is peculiar about the cartoons of Campbell is the way most of them portray her not as aspiring but as already in power and deserving comeuppance. In those by Gable she drives the powerful car. In Nipper's, she stands hands-on-hips, as if scolding. In an April 21 cartoon by King of *The Ottawa Citizen*, she confidently flies a make-believe helicopter.

After the shock and controversy around Campbell's "enemies," "SOB," and "to hell" remarks, this caricature of a scolding and arrogant Campbell intensified into one of narcissism and intolerance. Much like the journalists who portrayed these remarks as explicitly more intolerant than perhaps was warranted by the bare text of what Campbell had said, the cartoonists responded to the Major Douglas-like intolerance and carelessness of her remarks, and to the general vocabulary of impatience and prejudice she had unleashed. In the May 20 *Victoria Times-Colonist*, Raeside drew a map of "Kim Campbell's Canada." Instead of provinces, it had thirteen areas, variously labelled "Papal Demons," "Linguistically Challenged Jews," "Condescending SOBs," "Beer-Drinking Papists" — each of these an allusion to a Campbell phrase or claim; the geographic position of Ottawa was boldly labelled "Me." In a reference to the religious factionalism encouraged by an Irish rock singer, Corrigan in the May 23 *Toronto Star* portrayed a bald "Campbell" tearing in half a photograph of the Pope, and saying "Meet Sinéad O'Campbell." Gable in the May 27 *Globe and Mail* drew a self-pleased prima donna "Campbell," singing loudly to herself "I've gotta be MEEEE ..." while four of her "spin doctors" stood horrified on a ledge of a tall building ready to jump. The cartoon cleverly combined the already-circulating public associations of her with music, self-admiration, and refusal to take advice with a parody of her defence of her offending words, "I have a different way of expressing myself ... but I'm not prepared to be anything else" (in Winsor, "Media can't deal with candour, Campbell says"). In May 24's *Globe,* Jenkins drew a another beady-eyed "Campbell" pursued by hysterical, sign-waving supporters, shaking a voter's hand and saying "Pleased to meet you, you spotty little nonentity. I hope you'll get off your fat butt and vote for me come election day."

What all of these cartoons were depicting was a profound gap between "Campbell" and the surrounding figures. Her supporters were irrational and her advisors suicidal. The "tear" Corrigan showed her producing between the halves of the Pope's picture was also a tear in the Canadian social fabric. Her view of her own citizens was bullying and contemptuous.

■

> Vancouver Centre is home to one of Canada's largest — and most high-profile — gay and lesbian communities, whose leaders have vowed to unseat the defence minister. Gays and lesbians make up an estimated 20 per cent of the riding's 85,000 voters. Many of them complain that she let the community down by failing to recognize homosexual marriages in proposed amendments to the Canadian Human Rights Act. "The gay issue is big because of the sense of betrayal," says the NDP's Baxter, a lesbian activist. (*Maclean's,* 22 March 1993)

Feminist and lesbian feminist expressions of mistrust toward Campbell have depicted her generally as unsympathetic, out-of-touch, as being at best a feminist who does not carry her principles into action. Some of the feminists interviewed by Susan Riley for her article "Kim Campbell: Ms. Representing Feminism" could see Campbell only as

"Kim Campbell" the Tory. For them, to be Tory excluded the possibility of being feminist. Maude Barlow told Riley that a person could not belong to the Tories and not become like them "in character." "She sounds like some kind of feminist, but she is still carrying out the same politics of male dominance," said Shelagh Day of the National Action Committee on the Status of Women. "She comes across as a feminist, but she defends a neo-conservative agenda," said NAC's outgoing president, Judy Rebick.

These judgements probably explain the lack of feminist comment on the increasing isolation of Campbell within the Tory leadership race and on the increasing harshness of the attacks upon her. These attacks were not merely on Campbell but on a party of "male dominance"; when speaking her intolerant words, she was speaking not as a woman but as an agent of "a neo-conservative agenda." To be a feminist for Day, Barlow, and Rebick was to make one's experience of being a woman the basis of all of one's politics. (At the beginning of her article Riley herself defined a feminist as someone "who understand[s] that women's experience of life and politics is profoundly different from men's.") Such a feminist understands economics, law, education, family, international affairs, the environment, etc. first and foremost through her gender and her knowledge of how these fields and issues affect her and other women; she views women's oppression as collective rather than individual; she believes women to be helped more by general changes to attitudes, laws, and political institutions than by the success of individual women like Campbell. To work, as Campbell does, through a political party whose gendered, individualistic vision of these issues is overwhelmingly that of men, disqualifies her feminism. Her presence in the party merely gives additional credibility to a politics of personal initiative, entrepreneurial self-help, and "male dominance." To have worked earlier in a Social Credit party that had thrived on a divisive vocabulary of enemies and threat, of individual freedom versus creeping socialism, had associated her further with authoritarianism and middle-class self-interest. At the leadership convention, Campbell strengthened this association when she declared that she opposed the public funding of "advocacy groups"; for Campbell, as Jeffrey Simpson concluded in the *Globe* the day after the convention, "Capitalism ... best maximizes human freedom; state intervention does not necessarily enhance it."

Writing before the publication of Campbell's most abrasive remarks, Riley, like a few of the other feminists she interviewed, was ambivalent about Campbell. This ambivalence was evident in the punning subtitle of her article, "Ms. Representing Feminism?". Is Kim Campbell a Ms. who represents feminism, or is she a misrepresenter of feminism? Sunera Thobani (Riley spelled her name "Tobani"), and Unity Johnson of the National Organization for Immigrant and Visible Minority Women both express qualified admiration. Thobani tells Riley that while it is good to see a woman being "taken seriously by the media," she expects that Campbell will support "the most right-wing" of women's immigrant groups. When these women think of "Kim Campbell" they think of a woman who has won public acceptance but has nevertheless supported the purchase of military helicopters, supported a GST that has increased the household expenses of single-parent mothers, failed to champion a national day-care programme, and refused to argue for continued funding of the Charter of Rights Court Challenge Programme.

None of Campbell's feminist critics has commented on her characteristically female career pattern, or on the presence within it of obstacles women in our culture habitually encounter. On graduation from the University of B.C., Campbell did not immediately begin graduate study as a male student commonly does, but went with Divinsky, her future husband, to the University of Oregon where he was doing summer teaching. In the fall of that year, she returned with him to Vancouver and enrolled in a master's programme at UBC. In 1972-73 Divinsky spent his sabbatical in London where Campbell had enrolled two years earlier in doctoral studies at the London School of Economics. They married in 1973, and she gave up her studies to return to Vancouver at the end of his sabbatical year. What *Maclean's* will later call her subsequent "ricochet" career — part-time teaching, a law degree, political office — stems in part from the weak qualifications provided by this hodge-podge of postgraduate study, study marked by a woman's culturally limited freedom to choose the university at which she will study and to complete the programmes she does manage to enter. But what one can see here also is a pattern of very little apparent resistance to these career blockages, and even more the pattern noted earlier of a recurrent attraction to strong men — one that culminates in her expressions of "enormous respect" for Brian Mulroney. Her one protest about being treated unfairly as a woman during this period — that she was deprived of tenure-track teaching positions at Simon Fraser University and the University of British Columbia by departments that, in Newman's words, "seemed to regard political science as a man's discipline" — appears a weak one, considering that her only degree at the time was a B.A.

■

At another extreme, ideological conservatives both within and without the Conservative party have perceived a much different "Kim Campbell." This is a Campbell who is inexperienced, has risen too quickly, has not yet consistently demonstrated her views, and has shown alarming support for gay rights and feminist causes. This is *Alberta Report*'s Kim Campbell in "Less than meets the eye," a Campbell who "is everywhere called an intellectual, but has never been called upon to set forth either specific policies or a political philosophy." Such a Campbell even shows up from time to time in the mainly enthusiastic articles in the three 1993 "Campbell" issues of *Maclean's*. E. Kaye Fulton and Mary Janigan, the two reporters who write "The Real Kim Campbell" of the May 17 issue, hint that Campbell has enhanced her image — by "adroitly concealing details and editing facts" — and has even permitted the inflation of her academic credentials.

Throughout her leadership campaign *The Globe and Mail* was decidedly cool to Campbell. This coolness began with the editorial, "Kim Campbell, for all we know," published on the day she declared her candidacy. "She has just three years experience as a full minister in the cabinet," it complained; "as a campaigner, her track record is hardly enviable"; "on taxes, unemployment, inflation, education, health, social programs, *nada*." The cause of the paper's unhappiness was revealed only at the end of the editorial: Campbell is "solidly liberal" on social issues, "but stronger on the rights of groups than individuals." The coolness continued in the April 21 editorial "Campbell-babble," and in a number of columns by the *Globe*'s Edmonton correspondent, Kenneth Whyte, the western editor of the even more conservative *Saturday Night*.

Whyte's conservatism is of the populist kind. He defends the wisdom of voters, particularly western Canadian voters, to contribute to legislation, and looks skeptically at Campbell as an elitist who only pretends to value populist input. "Campbell shows that familiar tendency to blame the victim," he titled his April 3 column, and went on to argue that Campbell's early campaign speeches perpetuated "the hoary notion that responsibility for Canada's current problems lies mainly with the electorate." In the accusation of elitism was a hint of Major Douglas' suspicion of bankers and financiers. There were also echoes of Douglas' political theories, of their emphasis on the individual as the most important element in any society — but echoes somewhat different from any Campbell had produced. In Social Credit theory, Parliament is to serve and be controlled by its people, not by political parties — a position that diverges considerably from Campbell's scorn for citizens who do not participate in political parties. In his May 1 column, Whyte told the "crying-song" story of how Alberta-born country singer George Fox had been persuaded to accompany Campbell to the Juno Awards, but afterward was unable to get past Campbell aides to invite her to one of his shows. The import of the column was that Campbell had wantonly exploited Fox in order to create for herself a populist, "good ol' girl" image. "How a good ol' girl went courtin' the country vote," Whyte titled this column. "She reported on her date with George Fox and coquettishly encouraged a phantom rumour that there was something between them."

Whyte had made a similar critique of Campbell on March 20, nearly a week before Campbell's declaration of candidacy, in a column titled "Lucky Kim, she has the help of the same gang that doomed the accord." Here it was her unqualified support of the Charlottetown constitutional Accord that defined "Campbell" for him. It showed her involved not in a new politics but in "a politics of condescension." She was "thick with the old Mulroney gang." Her response to the Accord's defeat, expressed in a speech at Harvard University, had been unapologetically elitist: "[S]he argued that a major factor in the outcome was the ignorance of Canadians with regard to their own history and system of government. Canada does have a unique political culture, she said, but it is known only to the elite. She found it significant that the Yes voters tended to be well educated and affluent, decision-makers, people with what she called a feeling of civic competence." Again one can detect in Whyte an old-time Social Credit faith in the individual and suspicion of powerful elites. Cello-playing Campbell, with her admiration for the "well educated and affluent," was not sufficiently "Socred" for him.

In fact both Whyte's populism and the elitism of which he accused Campbell can be seen as strong anti-democratic forces. Elitism, as Whyte observes, asks the voter to suspend critical judgement and to trust in the analyses and opinions of experts. Populism, on the other hand, consists of knowledgeable people like Whyte, W.A.C. Bennett, Preston Manning, or the editors of *The Toronto Sun* flattering voters into thinking that they already know — that they are knowing individuals — and that they can have wisdom without work, debate, or inquiry. Populism stifles public debate by simplifying complex issues into slogans like "Say no to the Mulroney accord," and argues — again in the name of the individual — that the populace should have recall power over legislators, and referendum power over legislation. It opposes the "elitist" parliamentary notion of delegated authority. It pretends, like Whyte, not to be itself part of a power-possessing elite, but to be on the side of the "knowing" ordinary voter.

The coolness of the *Globe and Mail* toward Kim Campbell developed into near hostility as the June 11-13 Conservative convention approached. On June 9 it published the unsigned editorial, "On Balance, Jean Charest," in which it argued that the decisive difference between Campbell and Charest lay in her "unpredictability" and "brittleness" versus his "likeable demeanor." "For good or ill, there is less complexity to Mr. Charest." The *Globe*'s front-page stories of that week operated as a subtle extension of this editorial intervention. On June 8, it titled a largely sympathetic biographical article on Campbell by Stephen Brunt "Campbell's growing pains," offering thereby a jibe at the difficulty she was having in attracting additional delegate support. On June 9, in a story titled "Tories gear up for show time," it contrasted a Campbell convention programme of "Hollywood glamour and special effects" against a Charest one of "Mariposa folksiness." The *Globe*'s June 10 story headlined "Charest favoured in poll." Its June 11 front page featured a large photo of Brian Mulroney surrounded by "Kim!" campaign signs, and in a side bar described him as "the most loathed prime minister in Canada's history." The overall campaign view here largely duplicated that of Charest's more avid supporters: Campbell was an unstable woman ("unpredictable"); she was shallow ("Hollywood glamour") while he was a federalist and Canadian ("uncomplicated," "Mariposa folksiness"); he was his own man while she was in the pocket of a discredited Mulroney.

These attempts by the *Globe* to intervene as an institution (rather than a collection of individual editorial writers and columnists) in the Conservative campaign raises very difficult issues about party politics and democratic process. Does a Canadian political party — which is a much different constituency from the population in general (on which the *Globe*'s polls were based), and a decidedly more democratic institution than a Central Canadian newspaper with close ties to Bay Street — have the right, or power, to choose its own leader? Or does that power reside in a general population manipulated by a narrow barrage of media images? How democratic is a "free press" when it is dominated by one nationally circulated, small-c conservative paper, that can for days in a row place damaging images and stories about one candidate onto each delegate's breakfast table?

Decidedly more hostile than cool has been the populist-leaning *Alberta Report*. Its "Kim Campbell" is "left-wing, pro-gay, and pro-feminist." She has "mesmerized" a "doting media" with her "quick wit and left-of-centre opinions." In an insult only a western Canadian could fully understand, it suggested she has received "the most favourable press since Trudeau." Among the actions it found characteristic of "Campbell," it listed "the so-called 'rape-shield' law (another feminist-backed initiative)," her "half-hearted attempts to replace the abortion bill that was ruled unconstitutional by the Supreme Court," and a "surreptitious attempt to include homosexual rights in the Canadian Human Rights Act." As Riley commented in *This Magazine*, such a characterization makes her seem almost good enough for a feminist to support.

In actual fact, the policy proposals that Campbell put forward during the campaign were both more specific and more conservative than either the *Globe* or *Alberta Report* argued. Even her leadership convention speech, which much of the media deemed "flat" and "uninspiring," addressed many of the issues of the campaign — if not always openly, at least in codes familiar to Tory delegates. Like the words and images that have surrounded Campbell since her political debut in 1983, these codes gave extremely good indications of the kinds of policies a Campbell government would adopt:

1) *It would continue the fiscally conservative Mulroney agenda, and fit within Conservative Party traditions.* The second nominating endorsement of Campbell which prefaced the speech was Finance Minister Michael Wilson's emphatically overstated declaration that she had his "absolute support." In the speech itself, Campbell declared "that for one generation to run up a debt that

future generations will have to pay is morally wrong." She saluted Robert Stanfield, Joe Clark, and Brian Mulroney. The salute was ostensibly for their having opened the Conservative party to the participation of women, but the effect for delegates was to propose "Kim Campbell," the name whose way these men had opened, as the inheritor of an unbroken three-generation tradition of Tory policy. Toward the end of the speech she referred elliptically to the Mulroney government's policies such as free trade and the GST, and the need to preserve them, proclaiming that it would be "unfair to throw away all that has been gained by the hard sacrifice and difficult adjustments [Canadians] have made in recent years."

2) *A Campbell government would be in some ways even more publically conservative than the tradition it was inheriting*. One indicator of this was the fact that her opening sentence promised a continued "war against the deficit." Another was her allusion to the *immorality* of older generations running up debts for the younger — an indicator underlined by the three youth delegates, one each from Quebec, the Territories, and British Columbia, whose nomination endorsements also introduced her speech. A third was her insistence on newness: "I ask you now to support real change ... we can respond to the winds of change or we can be swept away." "Canadians want change," she declared at another point, "they deserve no less." One of the winds of change to which Campbell appeared to be alluding here was the perception across Canada in 1992-93 of a public debt crisis — a crisis which had led provincial governments, like those of Ontario's Bob Rae and Saskatchewan's Roy Romanow, to initiate drastic expenditure cutbacks, and which had allowed Newfoundland premier Clyde Wells to gain re-election on a platform of severe austerity. Coupled with the sign of "candour" which Campbell had also continued to claim, this allusion

seemed to promise a Wells-like campaign for Conservative re-election — a brutally frank campaign of fiscal bluntness in which Liberal, NDP, Reform, and Bloc Québécois opponents were all characterized as peddling economically ruinous fantasies. Conservatives, she announced, as she neared the end of her speech, must be ready "to face up to the hard facts of the 1990s."

3) *A Campbell government would replace constitutional and linguistic issues with gender issues.* The initial nominating endorsement of Campbell which had preceded the speech was delivered entirely in English by Ellen Fairclough, the first Canadian woman cabinet minister. Throughout the speech itself, Campbell practiced a rigourous "cereal-box" bilingualism, repeating almost every sentence in both French and English. Implicit in these alternating sentences was a Canada of two unilingualisms — each unilingualism able to understand only half of what Campbell was saying. The Trudeau vision of a bilingual Canada, in which francophones and anglophones would feel at home throughout the entire country (a vision implicit in many of Charest's "federalist" remarks) was here displaced by an older and once lamented "two solitudes." At the point in the speech when she spoke directly to the "woman" issue Fairclough's appearance had announced, Campbell repeated a quip she had used in the leadership debates: "our party is ready for a leader from *either founding gender.*" The quip ironically re-phrased the "two founding cultures" concept of Canada, one already somewhat discredited by First Nations' observation that they are as much a founding "culture" of Canada as francophones or anglophones. As a woman, Campbell had as much claim to the prime ministership as had Jean Charest as a Québécois. That is, Campbell was staking her claim to the leadership not by asserting her status as an anglophone against his status as a francophone, but by asserting the

paradigm of gender against the *paradigms* of language and linguistic culture. This assertion covertly continued a long-standing western Canadian grievance against bilingualism and biculturalism: just as Alberta is culturally more Ukrainian than francophone, Canada, Campbell's speech hinted, is culturally far more female than French.

4) *A Campbell government would attempt to convert income maintenance programmes like welfare or unemployment insurance into retraining programmes aimed at job creation.* This element of the Campbell speech was almost explicit rather than coded: speaking of job creation, she declared "our emphasis must be on skills training; if we do that, unemployment insurance and social assistance will be less about getting government cheques and more about getting paycheques." Welfare is to become workfare.

5) *A Campbell government would bring to federal politics the same ethical equation of small business and individualist moral values that was a bedrock principle of B.C. and Alberta Social Credit in the 1950s and 60s.* Again, this message was nearly explicit: "Driving that plan [for creating jobs] is small business, which we value in this party not only for its contributions to the economy but for the values it promotes: resourcefulness, independence, hard work."

Nevertheless, a day after this speech the *Globe*'s Jeffrey Simpson would still entitle his column: "The gnawing question: just who is she?"

■

> Her attitude of intellectual superiority was evident following the defeat of the Charlottetown accord in the October 26 referendum. She said that the deal had been defeated, not because Canadians rejected it on its merits but because the Yes coalition had failed to "educate" ordinary Canadians to grasp its many advantages. (*Alberta Report*, 29 March 1993)

One belief that has united left and right in their imaginative creations of "Kim Campbell" is that she is elitist, privileged, and over-educated. Class envy and anti-intellectualism can be found in both creations. Above, *Alberta Report* joined with the populism of Kenneth Whyte in arguing that the majorities that voted against the Charlottetown Accord referendum were necessarily "wiser" than the elites who drafted it. Elsewhere in this article, "Ordinary folk are nice but boring, says Kim," it mocked Campbell's claim to "genuinely like ordinary people," much like NDP organizers in Vancouver have continued to mock her 1983 attempt to reassure a skid row audience of her knowledge of disappointment by telling them of how she once wanted to be a concert cellist. The Alberta right associated her with an intellectual, urbane, and arrogant Trudeau. The middle-of-the road *L'actualité* associated her with an "arrogant, amusing ... certainly sexy Trudeau." NDP Member of Parliament Lynn Hunter told *Maclean's* sardonically that Campbell "is the only one I have ever heard [in Parliament] quote Plato. I mean, give me a break, Kim. This is the House of Commons, not academia." B.C. feminist New Democrats, according to Susan Riley, think of her as "a right-wing Socred, an abrasive school trustee, an arrogant advocate of privilege." Sometimes the class envy becomes expressed as outright ocular malice, as in Stan Persky's comment to *Maclean's'* Fulton and Janigan that Campbell, when a fellow student council member at the University of B.C. in the 1960s, "looked like a straight right-winger, well-dressed with fluffy blond hair. I thought, 'Oh God. Here's the ancient regime'."

In many of these cases it seems as if it is not particular signs and images with which Campbell has associated herself that are being responded to, but rather combinations of signs — clothing, politics, class, attitude, language, and education — in which any single sign can stand for the entire constellation.

■

The perception that most unites her critics, however, is that she has tended to antidemocratically transform politics into theatre or spectacle. "It is the style rather than the substance of Ms. Campbell's performance in the Charlottetown episode that is most ominous," Whyte wrote. "The pitch was all sentiment, no information." A vocabulary of studied drama and literary artifice — "style," "performance," "episode," "pitch" — runs through his comment. The *Maclean's* article that greeted her appointment to the defence portfolio called her a "quick-witted, cello-playing comedienne," and then recalled that when in law school at the University of B.C. she had been "the director of the school's annual amateur cabaret." The generally biographical articles of Vastel, Steed, and Fulton/Janigan all noted and lingered over moments when Campbell drew attention to herself with dramatic comments or gestures. Vastel told of her replying to Ian Waddell's suggestion that she "drop her intellectualism" with the rejoinder that in his case "that would not be difficult." Steed quoted Toronto lawyer Jane Pepino's account of Campbell's successfully competing with professional comedians at a Vancouver fundraiser:

> It was A Night at the Improv, a comedy club, and she blew me away. She improvised with two professional comics, it was a risk, and she flew with it. Then she did a 15 minute monologue, with a fabulous Joe Clark imitation, that had us rolling in the aisles.

Fulton and Janigan told of Campbell staging "impromptu cancans" before her Grade 8 classmates, organizing "skits for [her] high-school assemblies," and with her first husband "taking the male and female leads in impromptu performances of Gilbert and Sullivan operettas." For Fulton and Janigan, this flair for the theatrical led them to begin their article "Kim Campbell knew how to become a celebrity long before she knew how to be an effective politician," and to conclude by declaring that her "instinctive flair for self-promotion ... takes precedence over ... the need to do something." The first political incident they described in Campbell's life was her entering the Socred leadership convention on her lonely challenge of Bill Vander Zalm by herself, "behind a lone piper."

More hostile critics have characterized Campbell as someone who grandstands. In describing what he saw as her exploitation of George Fox, Kenneth Whyte wryly remarked that for western Canadian events she now "has a cowboy hat for when the cameras come round," and that it had "got her onto many a front page." In "Campbell-babble," the *Globe* pronounced her campaign "evasive and fundamentally manipulative of public opinion."

There are two disturbing aspects about "Campbell's" repeated association and self-association with theatricality — in addition to its troubling recollection of Pierre Elliott Trudeau. One is encapsulated in the slogan under which she proposed herself as a freshman candidate for the University of British Columbia student council almost thirty years ago, and recalled by Newman in his interview: "Kim is cuddlier." The slogan has appropriately vanished with her adolescence, but the cute image persists. The cute "Kim," what Newman describes as "perky, smart, sexy ... a beatific smile and blue eyes even Michael Wilson would drown in," now operates as a seductive and distracting cover for a large package of Conservative policies, both past and present, that are for most Canadians at best unfortunate, at worst repugnant. "Kim" is indeed cuddlier, cuddlier than the GST, than the widespread unemployment that has followed the Free Trade Agreement, than the higher provincial taxes that have been caused by federal reductions in transfer payments — much cuddlier indeed than military helicopters or than the medicare user fees that Campbell has announced herself ready to discuss. "Kim" is cuddlier than Brian, and has undoubtedly been supported by much of the Tory party because a cuddlier Brian has been in this pre-election period a specific Tory need. "Kim," in short, aestheticizes a whole range of unpopular Tory policies, substitutes for them a politics of spectacle — of flashing eyes, beatific smiles, cowboy hats, and daring one-liners. We roll in the aisles with the less cuddly Jane Pepino, rather than remember "Lyin' Brian" of "no free trade" and "sacred trusts."

Walter Benjamin has theorized that the transforming of politics into theatre and spectacle removes it from an arena of social discussion — where ideas can be proposed, weighed, disputed, and argued — into a arena of unthinking mass response. The beautiful spectacle, whether a mass rally or a seductive leader, overwhelms the viewer with an "aura" of mystery and authority. One of its ultimate expressions is the perception that weapons of war, and war itself, are beautiful. In Canada, the cult of the Avro Arrow and the mystique of our home-built navy carries much of that sense of the beautiful. And numerous Canadians, including myself, sat enraptured two years ago as the beautiful weapons dramatically entertained us from a "theatre of operations" in Iraq. In such a theatre, can a pragmatic, intelligent reassessment of Kim's helicopter, the charismatically powerful EH-101, even be considered?

The second disturbing aspect of Campbell's association with theatricality comes into focus with her quip to *Maclean's* reporters on assuming the defence portfolio: "Don't mess with me, I've got tanks." There is a discomforting dramatic pattern in the collection of offhand, joking, and I-didn't-really-mean-it remarks by which Campbell has recurrently fashioned herself for public view. In one she is the child of Daddy Warbucks — and we know how he makes his money. In another she is defending us against the "enemies" of Canadians — who turn out to be us. In another she is jokingly imagining herself sending out the tanks, against the reporters who may "mess" with her, the free press they represent, and ultimately against the people — us — that this free press speaks for. In yet another she is calling many of us "condescending SOBs" and wishing us "to hell." There is a repeating quality of anger, violence, intolerance, and arbitrary assertion in these outbursts. It could perhaps be civically useful, despite Benjamin's reservations, to have a flamboyant and theatrical leader, one who seduced other Canadians *into* political engagement, who made politics interesting, and whose offhand remarks were not only candid and charming but also joyful, thoughtful, and — to use a "Kim" term — "inclusive." But the signs around "Kim Campbell" — "Defiant Campbell" (*Toronto Star*, 24 May 1993), "Campbell opens fire" (*London Free Press*, 4 June 1993) — continue to present her as less thoughtful than even her school-teaching Anne of Green Gables precursor.

What, then, does the "Kim Campbell" name and prime-ministership mean? This book began with that question — not with whether the blonde, smiling, witty Kim Campbell was *well-meaning*, but with what the words, images, and actions associated with "Kim Campbell" might *mean* for Canadian voters. There have been too many "well-meaning," highly ideological contemporary democratic politicians — from Margaret Thatcher to Jimmy Carter — for sincerity, good intentions, or well-meaningness to be mistaken for wise, humane, or culturally enriched policy. The "Kim Campbell" signs often suggest things much different from well-meaningness — violence, intolerance, political polarization, anti-democratic manipulation, aggression, contempt — barely concealed beneath the seductive persona of a witty, entertaining, and even, it is reported, privately personable and charming politician. This politician has already — despite the ominous signs she displays — dazzled a relatively hard-headed Conservative party with her smile, humour, pluckiness, and little orphan heroism into giving her the leadership of the party. There is indeed powerful charisma here, but is it anything more than an ominous and self-serving substance that it covers? The appropriate words for "Kim Campbell" as she seeks the approval of both Tory bagmen and ourselves may be again those that Lucy Maud Montgomery gave to Anne: "I'll try to do and be anything you want me to, if you'll only keep me" (51).

Works Cited

Benjamin, Walter. "The Work of Art in the Age of Mechanical Reproduction." *Illuminations*. 1955. Tr. Harry Zohn. New York: Harcourt Brace Jovanovich, 1968.

Blodgett, E.D. *Configurations*. Downsview, ON: ECW Press, 1982.

Bowering, George. *Caprice*. New York: Viking, 1987.

Brunt, Stephen. "Campbell's growing pains." *Globe and Mail* 8 June 1993: A1, A8.

Camp, Dalton. "In tussle of Thobani let's not forget legacy of NAC's rude jousting." *Toronto Star* 16 May 1993: B3.

_____. "Only Campbell failed to meet expectations." *Globe and Mail* 18 April 1993: B3.

_____. "Tory hopefuls' choice: Be toady or be ingrate." *Toronto Star* 4 April 1992: B3.

"Campbellbabble." *Globe and Mail* 21 April 1993: A16.

"The candidates speak on the issues." *London Free Press* 1 May 1993: A8-9.

Cernetig, Miro. "Klein's PCs hardly PC." *Globe and Mail* 5 April 1993: A1.

_____. "Leadership hopefuls woo Alberta Tories." *Globe and Mail* 5 April 1993. A4.

"Clifford raises marital status as campaign issue." *London Free Press* 9 June 1993: A1, A3.

Couture, Pauline. "Charting the course of Campbellmania." *Globe and Mail* 1 April 1993: A23.

Cowie, Peter. *The Cinema of Orson Welles.* New York: Da Capo, 1973.

Crane, David. "It's wrong to saddle youth with diminished prospects." *Toronto Star* 8 May 1993: A2.

Desbarats, Peter. "Linguistic landmarks." *London Free Press* 8 May 1993: E3.

"Decriminalize Marijuana." *Toronto Star* 18 April 1993: B2.

Delacourt, Susan. "Campbell ready for medicare user fees." *Globe and Mail* 30 April 1993: A6.

Doyle, Patrick. "Campbell slams critics for 'apathy'." *Toronto Star* 18 May 1993. A1, A13.

_____. "Kim craze irks some PCs." *Toronto Star* 22 March 1993: A4.

"Fiery Campbell launched as a Tory." *Vancouver Sun* 19 October 1988: A1-2.

Finlay, John. *Social Credit: The English Origins.* Montreal: McGill-Queen's UP, 1972.

Foglia, Pierre. "Le gros con-sul." *La Presse* 15 April 1993: A5.

Fotheringham, Allan. "The View from behind the shoulders." *Maclean's* 22 March 1993: 50.

Fulton, E. Kaye, and Mary Janigan. "The Real Kim Campbell." *Maclean's* 17 May 1993: 16-23.

_____, et al. "The Rising Star." *Maclean's* 18 January 1993: 12-14.

Gagnon, Lysiane. "High Marks for Kim Campbell's first major foray into Quebec." *Globe and Mail* 3 April 1993: D3.

Galbraith, John Kenneth. "For many, recession is a nice thing." *London Free Press* 13 May 1993: B1.

Goar, Carol. "'Double standard' may work for Campbell." *Toronto Star* 12 June 1993: A1, A9.

Godbout, Jacques. *Knife on the Table.* 1965. Tr. Penny Williams. Toronto: McClelland and Stewart, 1968.

Gwyn, Richard. "Canada's Humpty-Dumpty politicians are in pieces." *Toronto Star* 18 April 1993: B3.

_____. "It all boils down to one factor, 'winnability'." *Toronto Star* 11 June 1993: A27.

Howard, Ross. "Campbell stands up for PM." *Globe and Mail* 20 May 1993: A5.

_____. "Campbell under gun in Calgary." *Globe and Mail* 26 April 1993: A3.

_____. "Front-runner taking the risk-free approach." *Globe and Mail* 8 April 1993: A4.

_____. "Lobbyists circle lobby-reform advocate." *Globe and Mail* 17 May 1993: A4.

Howse, John. "Backyard Challenges." *Maclean's* 22 March 1993: 20-21.

"I'm only human, Campbell says." *Toronto Star* 18 April 1993: A12.

"Just what was (and wasn't) said." *Globe and Mail* 19 May 1993: A9.

"Kim Campbell, for all we know." *Globe and Mail* 26 March 1993: A22.

Kipling, Rudyard. *Kim*. 1901. New York: Dodd Mead, 1962.

Kolodny, Annette. "A Map for Rereading: Gender and the Interpretation of Literary Texts." 1980. In David H. Richter, ed., *The Critical Tradition*. New York: St. Martin's Press, 1989. 1126-36.

Laurence, Margaret. *A Bird in the House*. 1963. Toronto: McClelland and Stewart, 1974.

"Le style Charest." *L'actualité* 1 May 1993: 25-6.

Lee, Robert Mason. "Are women politicians forced to make Sophie's choice?" *Vancouver Sun* 10 June 1993: A13.

Leishman, Rory. "A need for leadership." *London Free Press* 4 May 1993: B7.

_____. "Charest's qualities make him best choice." *London Free Press* 10 June 1993: B9.

"Less than meets the eye." *Alberta Report* 29 March 1993: 8-11.

"Liberals' copter plans more costly, Tory says." *Globe and Mail* 5 May 1993: A5.

Lortie, Marie-Claude. "Homicides en Somalie: l'opposition veut la démission de Kim Campbell." *La Presse* 23 April 1993: A4.

_____. "L'opposition torpille Kim Campbell dans l'affaire de meurtre en Somalie." *La Presse* 21 April 1993: A1.

MacQueen, Ken. "Campbell's frankness manipulated by news media." *London Free Press* 20 May 1993: B11.

Matas, Robert. "Campbell makes it official." *Globe and Mail*, 26 March 1993. A1.

"Mom, 18, rejected, pageant cancelled." *Toronto Star* 9 May 1993: A13.

Montgomery, Lucy Maud. *Anne of Green Gables.* 1908. Toronto: McGraw-Hill Ryerson, 1970.

"MP's questions racist, NAC says." *Globe and Mail* April 24, 1993: A6.

Nepveu, Pierre. *L'hiver de Mira Christophe.* Montreal: Boréal, 1986.

Newman, Peter C. "Citizen Kim." *Vancouver Magazine* May 1993: 28-38, 51-52, 91.

Oake, George. "Campbell faces fight in her own riding." *Toronto Star* 22 March 1993: A4.

_____. "On Balance, Jean Charest." *Globe and Mail* 9 June 1993: A20.

Parent, Rollande. "Charest's wife a veteran of many political campaigns." *London Free Press* 10 May 1993: A3.

"PC Leadership Notebook." *London Free Press* 10 May 1993: A3.

Picard, André. "Charest works hard to come out of his shell." *Globe and Mail* 5 June 1993: A1, A6.

Poulin, Jacques. *Volkswagen Blues.* 1984. Toronto: McClelland and Stewart, 1988.

Powe, B.W. *The Solitary Outlaw.* Toronto: Lester & Orpen Dennys, 1987.

Pugliese, David. "Campbell faces fire: Minister put on Defense over handling of Somali killings." *Calgary Herald* 24 April 1993: A1.

Riley, Susan. "Ms. Representing Feminism? The Troubling Ascent of Kim Campbell." *This Magazine* May 1993: 11-15.

Rossiter, Sean. "Free speaker: Kim Campbell's political rise is marked by moves like breaking Socred ranks over abortion." *Vancouver Magazine* April 1988: 34-35.

Sellar, Don. "Campbell between the lines." *Toronto Star* 22 May 1993: D2.

Sheppard, Robert. "Reach for the Top: campaign edition." *Globe and Mail* 24 March 1993: A19.

Simpson, Jeffrey. "The gnawing question: just who is she?" *Globe and Mail* 14 June 1993: A15.

Speirs, Rosemary. "Campbell unfazed as Clark backs Charest." *Toronto Star* 8 June 1993: A1.

_____. "'Outsiders' are okay in Canada." *Toronto Star* 8 May 1993: D1, D4.

Steed, Judy. "In pursuit of power. Kim Campbell: a portrait." *Toronto Star* 1 May 1993: D1, D4-6.

Stewart, Edison. "Taking the new politics to the forest." *Globe and Mail* 13 May 1993: A25.

_____. "Won't meddle in debate on sign law: Campbell." *Toronto Star* 20 April 1993: A10.

"The Tattler." *Globe and Mail* 10 May 1993: A2.

"Tories gear up for show time." *Globe and Mail* 9 June 1993: A1.

Valpy, Michael. "Misrepresenting Kim Campbell." *Globe and Mail* 19 May 1993: A2.

Vastel, Michel. "L'effet Campbell." *L'actualité* 1 May 1993: 20-24 (Most passages translated by author).

Ward, John. "Estimates to rebuild 'copters labelled too high." *Toronto Star* 14 May 1993: A9.

Whyte, Kenneth. "Campbell shows that familiar tendency to blame the victim." *Globe and Mail* 3 April 1993: D2.

_____. "How a good ol' girl went courtin' the country vote." *Globe and Mail* 1 May 1993: D2.

_____. "Lucky Kim, she has the help of the same gang who doomed the accord." *Globe and Mail* 20 March 1993: D2.

_____. "Official bilingualism has failed to achieve its true purpose." *Globe and Mail* 8 May 1993: D2.

Wilson, Deborah. "Heir to NAC stung by attack." *Globe and Mail* 10 May 1993: A1-2.

Wilson-Smith, Anthony, and Luke Fisher. "In Mulroney's Grip." *Maclean's* 29 March 1993: 10-11.

_____. "Why is this woman smiling?" *Maclean's* 22 March 1993: 12-15.

Winsor, Hugh. "Candidates not ready for prime time." *Globe and Mail* 16 April 1993: B3.

_____. "Charest favoured in poll." *Globe and Mail* 10 June 1993: A1, A4.

_____. "Media can't deal with candour, Campbell says." *Globe and Mail* 26 May 1993: A1-2.

_____. "Segal shied at starting gate." *Globe and Mail* 9 April 1993: A1.

_____. "Warm, funny side of Campbell being served up." *Globe and Mail* 26 March 1993: A4.

York, Geoffrey. "Charest comes out swinging." *Globe and Mail* 14 May 1993: A4.

____. "Forget Fees, Tories warned." *Globe and Mail* 13 May 1993: A1-2.